T0328705

Cambridge Elements

Elements in New Religious Movements
Series Editor
Rebecca Moore
San Diego State University
Founding Editor
†James R. Lewis
Wuhan University

THE CHRISTIAN COUNTERCULT MOVEMENT

Douglas E. Cowan
Renison University College

CAMBRIDGE
UNIVERSITY PRESS

Shaftesbury Road, Cambridge CB2 8EA, United Kingdom

One Liberty Plaza, 20th Floor, New York, NY 10006, USA

477 Williamstown Road, Port Melbourne, VIC 3207, Australia

314–321, 3rd Floor, Plot 3, Splendor Forum, Jasola District Centre,
New Delhi – 110025, India

103 Penang Road, #05–06/07, Visioncrest Commercial, Singapore 238467

Cambridge University Press is part of Cambridge University Press & Assessment,
a department of the University of Cambridge.

We share the University's mission to contribute to society through the pursuit of
education, learning and research at the highest international levels of excellence.

www.cambridge.org
Information on this title: www.cambridge.org/9781009054171

DOI: 10.1017/9781009053419

First published 2023

A catalogue record for this publication is available from the British Library.

ISBN 978-1-009-05417-1 Paperback
ISSN 2635-232X (online)
ISSN 2635-2311 (print)

The Christian Countercult Movement

Elements in New Religious Movements

DOI: 10.1017/9781009053419
First published online: July 2023

Douglas E. Cowan
Renison University College

Author for correspondence: Douglas E. Cowan, decowan@uwaterloo.ca

Abstract: Many seemingly strange questions on yoga, salvation, religious pluralism, and so forth have been actively debated among members of a small but influential group of evangelical apologists known as the Christian countercult movement. This Element explores the history of this movement from its origins in the anti-heresy writings of the early church to its modern development as a reaction to religious pluralism in North America. It contrasts the apologetic Christian countercult movement with its secular anticult counterpart and explains how faith-based opposition both to new religious movements and to non-Christian religions will only deepen as religious pluralism increases. It provides a concise understanding of the two principal goals of Christian countercult apologetics: support for the evangelization of non-Christian believers and maintenance for the perceived superiority of the evangelical Christian worldview.

Keywords: countercult, apologetics, cults, new religions, anticult

ISBNs: 9781009054171 (PB), 9781009053419 (OC)
ISSNs: 2635-232X (online), 2635-2311 (print)

Contents

Introducing the Christian Countercult

'The only reason for becoming familiar with other religions and other religious writings', declared the Christian apologist Dave Hunt in 1996, 'would be in order to show those who follow these false systems wherein the error lies and thereby to rescue them' (68). Lest one protest that these sentiments violate the United States' vaunted – not to mention constitutionally enshrined – commitment to religious freedom, conservative evangelicals John Ankerberg and John Weldon answer the charge in their *Encyclopedia of Cults and New Religions*. That is, since a 'solidly Christian' America 'seems to have been the divine plan . . . the First Amendment only works as long as we accept Christian principles' (1999: xxix). Take a moment to read that last part again and ponder its implications. More than that, they continue, 'if it does not', which is to say, if American guarantees of religious freedom are not anchored in evangelical Christianity, 'then it gets what it gets – all kinds of religious evils protected by the very amendment which God intended to bless the nation' (xxix). Among these putative evils, warned Walter R. Martin, indeed 'of all the major cults extant in the melting pot of religions called America, none is more subtle or dangerous to the unwary soul than the Church of Jesus Christ of Latter-day Saints' (1980: 63), which Martin called elsewhere 'a polytheistic nightmare of garbled doctrines draped with the garments of Christian terminology' (1985: 226), and whose theology he condemned as 'a blasphemous derivation from the mythology of Greece coupled with unmistakable signs of pagan sexual perversions' (1976: 27).

Known throughout his long career as 'the Bible Answer Man' and considered by many to be the father of modern countercult apologetics, Walter Martin died in June 1989. Though at that point I had no idea who he was, his death occurred less than a week before I was to take up my position as the United Church of Canada minister on a small pastoral charge nestled in the rolling hills and mixed farmland around Cardston, Alberta. To this day I remember the conversation during which I learned of my new posting. After the usual pleasantries, the denominational official paused, then asked in a low tone, 'How do you feel about . . . interfaith dialogue?' 'Fine', I replied carefully, a little confused by the question. After all, I was newly ordained in one of the most liberal Protestant denominations in North America. For us, inter-religious dialogue was all but an article of faith. What could he possibly mean?

'Why?' I asked.

'Well', he said, not a hint of irony in his voice, 'there are some Mormons there'.

As some readers may know, Cardston and its less-populous neighbours, Spring Coulee and Magrath, constituted the northern line of Latter-day Saint

(LDS) advance in the late 1880s as they sought to escape newly enacted federal anti-polygamy laws in the United States. As it grew, Cardston became not only the first Temple city in Canada, but a hub for Mormon immigration and expansion into that country. By the time I arrived, 100 years after those first Mormon settlers, of the town's roughly 5,000 inhabitants well over 90 percent identified as Latter-day Saints, and it was said that there were more LDS missionaries per capita in Cardston than anywhere else in the world. Dominating the townscape, the Cardston temple had just undergone a spectacular renovation. The various LDS stake centres were by far the largest and most numerous local houses of worship in the area. And, in both Alberta and Utah, Cardston was known colloquially as 'Salt Lake City North'. But, curiously, it is also the only place I have ever lived where people often identify themselves initially by what they are not. 'Hi, the name's Bob; I'm *not* Mormon' was a common way for non-LDS people to introduce themselves to me, not infrequently with a subtle wink and a tacit nod.

Knowing virtually nothing about Latter-day Saints before I moved to my new pastoral charge, I visited a Christian bookstore in my hometown on Vancouver Island. After explaining my situation, I was handed what the clerk assured me was 'the best book on the topic': Dave Hunt and Ed Decker's infamous *The Godmakers* (1984). I recall saying to my mother, as I was leafing through it a few days later, 'Mom, they're sending me to Mars.' The world Hunt and Decker described was an alien one indeed. Strange and secretive rituals, magical underwear, the ongoing practice of polygamy, the quest to become gods of their own planet, all of this and more combined with the remarkable claim that Latter-day Saints 'take more non-barbiturate sedatives, tranquilizers, antidepressants, stimulants, pep pills, heroin, cocaine and LSD than non-Mormons' (Hunt and Decker 1984: 19). Reading *The Godmakers* made it seem as though I was headed for some kind of weird, hedonistic, junkie paradise. Of course, it wasn't that way at all.

Most of the Latter-day Saints I met there were friendly, and for the five years I lived in Cardston, they appeared to me relentlessly normal as they went about their lives. Some were better than others. Some worked hard, others less so. Some of their kids were well behaved, others, well, not so much. In short, apart from their religious beliefs, they were just like anybody else. Though recognizing that I was 'different', many of them went out of their way to make me feel welcome in their community. More conspiracy-minded folks in my own congregation were convinced that this overt show of affection was nothing more than a tactic aimed at recruiting the new minister, but that never seemed the case to me. In fact, I suspect that the proprietor of the local Latter-day Saint bookshop retains the distinction of having the only store anywhere in the world to stock copies of my first book (Cowan 1991) – most of which undoubtedly remain on the shelves to this day. And I never once saw evidence of heroin, cocaine, or LSD.

My point here is that I was so struck by the disparity between Hunt and Decker's hostile, pugnacious description of Mormonism and my experience in this profoundly LDS enclave that I began to collect materials similar to theirs from evangelical bookstores and churches across southern Alberta. I wanted to understand this strange obsession with the dangerous religious Other, and I was astonished at just how much of it there was and how deeply ingrained it is in evangelical culture. I found not only anti-Mormon material, but anti-Jehovah's Witness, anti-New Age, anti-Hindu, anti-Buddhist, anti-Pagan, anti-Catholic, indeed anti-just about any religion you could name. Gradually, a picture emerged of a conservative, mainly Protestant subculture dedicated to defending its narrow vision of the Christian faith against any and all competitors. Eventually, this collection grew to include the many hundreds of books, magazines and journals, news articles, pamphlets and tracts, broadsheets and one-off polemics, newsletters, audio- and videotapes, and, later, the rambling plethora of Internet shovelware – material that is simply replicated from website to website – that became the data set informing both my doctoral dissertation and much of my early academic work (Cowan 1999, 2002, 2003a, 2003b). All of which brings us to this Element.

'Strange as it may seem', Dave Hunt wrote in *The Cult Explosion*, the first of his more than thirty books on the topic, 'most cults are basically the same' (1980: 19). Arguing a position that only hardened over the course of his career, and which is still shared by those whose Christian identity is shaped at least as much by their opposition to other religious traditions as by devotion to their own, Hunt concludes that 'in spite of the apparently wide differences among the many cults, beneath the surface they all rest on a common foundation: the four lies Satan used to trick Eve' (19). According to Hunt at least, these are (a) the human possibility of godhood, (b) the rejection of moral absolutes, (c) a denial of death, and (d) that 'knowledge was the key to godhood and immortality' (110). Epitomizing the Christian countercult worldview, he concludes: 'There is an undeniable point-by-point correlation between these four premises of the serpent's philosophy and the basic ideas underlying not only paganism-occultism but also modern science, psychology, sociology, and every human religion. The odds against this happening by chance are too astronomical to calculate' (110). Indeed, for Hunt and hundreds of other countercult apologists, both lay and professional, whether well organized or entirely ad hoc, 'Satan is the author of every cult and false religion, and his imprint is clearly seen on them all' (239).

For most of those populating my growing library of source material, new, alternative, and emergent religions were clear evidence, for example, of *The Culting of America* (Rhodes 1994). The increasing presence of other world faiths highlighted the problem of *Alien Gods on American Turf* (Muck 1990). Some countercult apologists asked *Have You Witnessed to a Mormon Lately?* (Spencer 1986), while others warned darkly about sinister *Angels of Deceit* (Lee and Hindson 1993) and *Satan's 'Evangelistic' Strategy for This New Age* (Lutzer and DeVries 1989).

It is worth remembering that, at its most basic level, religion is always and everywhere a matter of perception and perspective, and that this is especially the case when exclusive faith claims and matters of cosmic consequence are at stake. What is seen depends on who is looking, what they are looking at, and the lenses through which they survey the cultural landscape around them. As I have pointed out elsewhere, 'this may seem an obvious insight, but it's astonishing how frequently it's forgotten. We so often seem to think that the way *we* see the sacred, if we claim to see it at all, is the way *everyone* sees it' (Cowan 2020: 7). Or, more to the point, the way everyone *should* see it if they know what's good for them.

Welcome to the evangelical Christian countercult.

Put simply, as I describe it in this Element, the Christian countercult is a relatively small, but surprisingly influential apologetics movement that exists largely within conservative evangelical Protestantism. Although minor variants exist within Roman Catholicism and Eastern Orthodoxy, particularly in Europe and Russia, the vast majority of modern countercult material is rooted in scriptural and doctrinal interpretations that go back in spirit, if not always in denominational lineage, to *The Fundamentals*, the twelve-volume collection of essays defending Protestant Christianity published in the United States between 1910 and 1915.

Even today, if you go into virtually any Christian bookstore (whether bricks-and-mortar or online) and search the shelves labelled 'Cults and Sects', 'Other Faiths', or 'World Religions', you will find many of the sources that I used more than twenty years ago still in print and prominently displayed, often in revised and updated editions. Evangelical scholar Douglas Groothuis, for instance, continues to insist on the importance of *Confronting the New Age*, just one of his books explaining 'how to resist [this] growing religious movement' (1988; see Groothuis 1986, 1990). James Bjornstad, on the other hand, still cautions Christians about the religious *Counterfeits at Your Door* (1979), while Robert Morey provides ongoing advice on *How to Answer a Jehovah's Witness* (1980), but more recently asks *Is Eastern Orthodoxy Christian?* (2015). By now, I imagine you can guess his answer. Similarly, in *Hidden Dangers of the*

Rainbow, Constance Cumbey warns anyone who will listen about 'the New Age Movement and Our Coming Age of Barbarism' (1983), while in *Demon-Proofing Prayers*, freelance exorcist Bob Larson offers his own patented 'guide to winning spiritual warfare' (2011). For his part, Walter Martin produced multiple editions of his magnum opus, *Kingdom of the Cults*, first published in 1965, but which, more than thirty years after his death, continues to appear in revised editions as 'the definitive work on the subject' (2019; see also Martin, Rische, and van Gorden 2008). Online, virtual iterations of such long-standing countercult groups as the Religious Analysis Service (RAS; www.ras.org), Spiritual Counterfeits Project (www.scp-inc.org), Evangelical Ministries to Non-Christian Religions (EMNR; www.emnr.org), Watchman Fellowship (WF; www.watchman.org), and the venerable Christian Research Institute, which Martin founded in 1960 (CRI: www.equip.org), still patrol the battlements, constantly on guard for the encroaching religious Other.

The Road Ahead

Whether they pursue countercult apologetics as a profession or as an avocation, whether they are focused on one particular group or regard the entire multi-religious landscape with existential alarm, whether they are part of an organized movement or follow their passion for the most part alone and online, evangelical countercult apologists regard any religious belief, practice, or faith tradition – from alternative interpretations of the Christian message (e.g., Freed 1980; Watters 1987) to different religions altogether (e.g., Hunt 1998a; Matrisciana 1985) – as both a threat to the validity and security of their own worldview, and as a 'problem of practical life' in terms of the ironclad mandate of the Great Commission (Matthew 28:16–20; see Mannheim 1952).

However, despite its popular emergence in North America after the Second World War, the countercult as a reaction to religious competitors is hardly a new phenomenon. As such, Section 1 of this Element places the modern movement in broad historical context as one ripple in a stream of Christian antipathy dating back as far as the early church, but finding its more precise antecedents in the nineteenth century. Following this, Section 2 briefly outlines countercult development in the twentieth century, particularly its post-war institutionalization and, in some cases, professionalization. By the end of the 1990s, the appearance of the World Wide Web had changed the nature of the countercult yet again, providing for a democratization of Christian apologetics that believers before that time could scarcely have imagined. Christian countercult organizations and ministries exist in many countries around the world, and share a common purpose in defending their own faith, most often through apologetic critique and proactive evangelization of other faiths, but occasionally by means of outright attack (see, e.g., Di Marzio 2020; Fautré 2020a, 2020b). This Element will mainly consider the countercult as it has developed in North America.

It is important to note, however, that evangelical Christian concern has not been the only response to the emergence of new and what many regard as questionable religious movements. Beginning in the late 1960s, a secular anti-cult movement quickly became the popular face of new religious opposition, largely because of its fearmongering proclamations and outré tactics. Although they are often considered part of the same social response to alternative religious groups, the secular anticult movement (ACM) and the Christian counter-cult movement (CCM) are, in fact, very different from each other and approach the problem of new religions in very diverse ways. 'Broadly put, the secular ACM proceeds according to different versions of the "brainwashing" or "thought-control" hypothesis and takes as its point of departure allegations of physical and mental abuse, attacking a number of nontraditional religious groups on the basis of alleged violations of civil liberties' (Cowan 2002: 340; see Introvigne 2022b). The Christian countercult, on the other hand, opposes new and alternative religious movements 'not primarily because of their alleged recruiting and retention methods, but because of their ontology, not by virtue of their presumed (anti-)social behaviour, but simply by virtue of their existence' (Cowan 2002: 340). Thus, Section 3 parses the difference between anticult and countercult in terms of their underpinning epistemologies, their respective apologetic methods and tactics, and their desired outcomes. Though both movements identify their religious opponents as cults, what they mean by that term, how they arrive at a determination about whether this group or that constitutes a cultic threat, and what they think should be done about it are very different – and should not be confused.

Section 4 discusses the modern Christian countercult in terms of its sociology of knowledge, as an extended exercise in evangelical worldview maintenance that has at least the potential for significant social impact. In the first instance, despite its often grandiose claims to front-line action in the face of new religious competition, the Christian countercult is largely a movement internal to evan-gelicalism, one that is often less concerned with converting others than with reinforcing the correctness of its own religious vision and thereby propagating an ongoing prejudice against any faith but its own. Despite the popularity of such series as the Zondervan Guide to Cults and Religious Movements (e.g., Hawkins 1998; Mather and Nichols 1995; Passantino and Passantino 1995; Yamamoto 1998) or apologist Ron Rhodes' numerous *Reasoning from the Scriptures with* [insert problematic religion here] books (e.g., 1993, 1995, 2000, 2001), the reality is that very few of the evangelical believers who consume countercult material will interact with new religion adherents in any meaningful way. Despite innumerable stand-alone volumes ranging from *Confronting the Cults* (Lewis 1966) and *Cult-Proofing Your Kids* (Martin 1993) to *When Cultists Ask* (Geisler and Rhodes 1997) and *Right Answers for Wrong Beliefs* (Slick 2002), evangelicals may 'cult-proof' their children, but they will rarely if ever 'confront the cults' directly or be placed in situations where 'cultists ask' them for anything other than directions. Rather, for these believers, countercult literature serves a different purpose altogether: it demonstrates in no uncertain terms the unimpeachable superiority of their own religious worldview, but does so by pointing out what it regards as the fatal flaws in all religions other than their own. Through the consumption of countercult apologetics, evangelical believers remain convinced that they have all the 'right answers' for any kind of 'wrong belief'.

This is not to say, however, that the Christian countercult has had no social impact. A number of countercult groups, for example, have promoted events intended to confront what they consider harmful religions, including protesting at the opening of new LDS temples or Scientology buildings, organizing weekend workshops that conclude with witnessing trips to this new religion or that, or sponsoring a variety of call-in radio programmes and podcasts. Works such as *The Godmakers* do not exist in a vacuum.

Prior to co-writing *The Godmakers* with Dave Hunt, Ed Decker, a Latter-day Saint who converted to evangelical Christianity in 1976, produced a short film, also titled *The God Makers*. (Note: although there is inconsistent usage across the countercult and relevant media, *The Godmakers* refers to the Hunt and Decker text, *The God Makers* to the Decker film.) Onscreen interviews with ex-Mormons and anti-Mormon apologists, animated lampoons of LDS theology and ritual, and dire warnings about the manifold dangers presented by the church frame a fictionalized class action lawsuit Decker and his fellow apostates hope to bring for what they see as 'fraud', 'deliberate misrepresentations', and 'causing family break-ups' (Decker 1982). According to one reporter at the time, '*The Godmakers* [*sic*], a 56-minute film produced by a group of former Mormons, has fueled claims of "religious pornography", as well as a wave of threats, harassment and violence in many of the places it has been shown, including Idaho where a fourth of the state's residents are Mormon' (Bossick 1983: 5). Decker himself claimed at the time that *The God Makers* was 'being shown more than a thousand times each month, with an average attendance of 2,500 people at each showing, or about 250,000 viewers per month' (Bossick 1983: 6). Setting aside Bossick's faulty maths, Decker is actually claiming that *The God Makers* was seen by two and a half *million* people every month. To put that in perspective, according to Decker, in the year following its release *The*

God Makers was seen by more people in one month than many high-budget Hollywood films during their entire theatrical run.

Decker's clear and slightly ridiculous exaggeration notwithstanding, the film was marketed to churches throughout the United States and, not surprisingly, generated a considerable number of complaints. After a months-long investigation, the National Conference of Christians and Jews (NCCJ) declared rather anticlimactically that Decker's film 'does not – in our opinion – fairly portray the Mormon Church, Mormon history, or Mormon beliefs'. That said, the NCCJ also criticized *The Godmakers* [sic] for its 'extensive use of "half-truths", faulty generalizations, erroneous interpretation, and sensationalism', finding 'particularly offensive the emphasis in the film that Mormonism is some sort of subversive plot – a danger to the community, a threat to the institution of marriage, and is destructive to the mental health of teenagers'. The letter concludes that, because '*The Godmakers* [sic] relies heavily on appeals to fear, prejudice and other less worthy human emotions', the 'continued use of this film poses genuine danger to the climate of good will and harmony' (National Conference of Christians and Jews 1984). Yet, nearly forty years after its release, a recent featured review on Amazon's Internet Movie Database, a standard online reference for all things cinema, television, and video game, warns that 'it is incredible all the crazy stuff that Mormons teach and it is frightening to see what they can do to you if you try to escape from them once your'e [sic] in their group. Do not trust Mormons, be afraid' (Leakhead 2020).

Section 5 of this Element considers the future of the Christian countercult which, unlike its secular counterpart, shows no signs of declining or fading away. Indeed, the situation is quite the opposite and for readily understandable reasons. Many of the books produced by prominent countercult apologists of the 1980s and 1990s are being reprinted or released in specialized e-book format. Many of these 'movement intellectuals' (Eyerman and Jamison 1991) – as well as those who have been influenced by them and, in some cases, have taken up their apologetic mantle – continue to write, publish, and speak publicly, responding now to such diverse threats as Islam (considered by many the fastest-growing religion worldwide) and atheism (one of the fastest-growing demographics among secular nations; e.g., DeStefano 2018; Hahn 2010; McFarland 2012; Miller 2012).

As liberal secular democracies become more diverse, both culturally and religiously, conservative evangelicals will feel increasing apologetic pressure to reinforce the infallible and insuperable nature of their own faith. In this respect, both 1 Peter 3:15, in which Jesus' followers are enjoined to 'always be prepared to give an answer to everyone who asks you to give the reason for the hope that you have', and Jude 1:3, urging believers 'to contend earnestly for the faith', will continue to carry at least as much weight as the Great Commission (Matthew 28:16–20). Despite the Covid-19 pandemic, for instance, EMNR (which changed its name in 2022 from Evangelical Ministries to *New Religions*) continues to produce yearly conferences at which many of the same people share many of the same stories, making the same apologetic arguments in the face of the same supposed religious threats.

To understand the modern evangelical CCM, it is necessary to look nearly two millennia back to the beginnings of what would eventually become the Christian church, a global religious phenomenon that accounts for more than one in every four people around the world.

1 The Christian Countercult in Historical Perspective

Although it has a number of significant antecedents, the Christian countercult as I describe it here came to prominence mainly under the force of multireligious expansions in the West following World War II. In Britain, for example, the Witchcraft Act of 1735 was repealed in 1951, replaced by the more specific Fraudulent Mediums Act, a decision that, among other things, cleared the way for self-declared modern Pagans to step out of the broom closet and into the public square, allowed for the publication of such books as Gerald Gardner's *Witchcraft Today* (1954), and eventually led to an increase in general interest in witches, witchcraft, and Wicca (see Ankarloo and Clark 1999; Berger 2005; Cowan 2005b; Hutton 2019). Across the pond, concern that Christian dominance was waning led to incorporation of the RAS in 1946, the principal mandate of which was to 'provide a *comprehensive and aggressive* specialized service, denominationally unrelated, designed to *enlighten and safeguard uninformed and unwary* individuals and groups against those false teachings which definitely prevent men from finding the saving grace that is obtainable alone through faith in the Lord Jesus Christ' (Religious Analysis Service, n.d.; emphasis added). Nearly two decades later, the 1960s saw the repeal of profoundly racist statutes which, to that point, had limited immigration from a specific group of countries, notably in Southern and Eastern Europe and Asia. This new openness invited a host of religious immigration and entrepreneurship, which provided competition for Christianity, to that point the virtually unchallenged faith tradition in the United States. Riding the wave of various countercultural movements, both America and Europe witnessed an explosion of alternative Christianities, novel interpretations of the faith that rejected the staid preaching of the past and sought to reach younger audiences with more relevant gospel messaging (see Lucas and Robbins 2004; Miller 1995). While many of these groups were swiftly condemned as cults, they all addressed what leaders and adherents alike saw as the patent failures of the traditional Christian church. None of this, however, should suggest that the issues with which countercult apologists concerned themselves had not been around for much, much longer than that.

A Brief History of Christian Antipathy

What does 'real' Christianity mean? Who are the 'true' Christians? Under what conditions can one claim 'legitimate' allegiance to the Son of God? And what are we to do about those who profess such fealty falsely? Beyond that, how should those who follow the one true God – and insist that all others do so as well – respond to the plethora of different spiritual visions spilling out from the human religious imagination? Questions such as these have vexed Christians almost since the inception of the church and not only driven the development of increasingly sophisticated theological apologetics, but also contributed to some of the most turbulent and consequential geopolitical developments of the past two millennia. Indeed, the history of Christian antipathy towards competing interpretations of the faith itself, as well as the glut of alternative traditions crowding the religion marketplace, goes back to the very beginning of Christian community.

Acts 15 and Galatians 2, which scholars consider complementary (though not identical) accounts of the same event, describe competing visions of Christian identity and church membership that occurred within just two decades of Jesus' death. According to the biblical texts, some leaders of the nascent church were adamant that adherence to principles laid down in the Torah – and for men, at least, manifest in the rite of circumcision – were requirements for inclusion in the Christian faith. Absent these, believers could not call themselves followers of Christ. Indeed, 'unless you are circumcised', Antiochene believers were told, and the ritual performed 'according to the custom taught by Moses, you cannot be saved' (Acts 15:1). Paul, the fiery convert from Tarsus and celebrated apostle to the Gentiles, objected sharply. Thus, at the Council of Jerusalem, dated to around 50 CE and often considered the first of Christianity's major ecumenical gatherings, the decision was made to require no more of non-Jewish converts than 'to abstain from food sacrificed to idols, from blood, from the meat of strangled animals, and from sexual immorality' (Acts 15:29). While the intervening 2,000 years may have blunted somewhat the theological force of this particular debate, it's worth noting that the central issue was soteriological: who could be part of the Kingdom of God and, more importantly, who was to be excluded.

Consider just a few of the more well-known versions of this same basic argument – quarrels, debates, even all-out armed conflicts that have fractured the Christian church from its earliest centuries to the present day. While the specific details may vary, the core of each involves central theological questions of who gets to call him/herself a Christian, who gets to decide the boundaries of the church, and on what grounds.

In *Prescription against the Heretics*, the early Christian polemicist Tertullian argued for the doctrine of apostolic succession as a way of securing what he considered necessary Christian orthodoxy against the variety of pagan influences extant in the region. Later in his own life, of course, Tertullian himself was roundly criticized for his adoption of an arch-moralist Montanism, a reaction to what he regarded as the liberalizing tendencies of many of his fellow Christian believers. In *Against Heresies*, Tertullian's contemporary, Irenaeus, condemned a variety of competing interpretations of the Christ event, its aftermath, and what that meant for membership in the Christian community. Chapter eight, for example, which exposes 'how the Valentinians pervert the Scriptures to support their own pious opinions', reflects almost exactly the principal means by which modern countercult apologists deride and dismiss any biblical exegesis that does not conform to their own. As for Augustine, in addition to his well-known antipathy towards Pelagius and his followers, he particularly attacked the heresy to which he once belonged, the Manichaeans (Smith 2021: 1; see also Bauer 1971; Cameron 2003; Lüdemann and Janssen 1997; Pagels 1989). Here, one of the most influential of the early Christian theologians mirrors the place both of the ex-member and of the anecdotal atrocity in precisely the same social construction of religious enmity we find in modern countercult apologetics. Although the quintessential Christological heresy, Arianism, emerged by the end of the third century, despite determined efforts at its eradication, it continued to appear throughout the millennium and a half that followed (see Williams 2001). Indeed, in 1846, Methodist Episcopal pastor Hiram Mattison watched with alarm what he considered the erosion of the principal theological tenet of Christianity, and published *A Scriptural Defence of the Doctrine of the Trinity, or, A Check to Modern Arianism, As Taught by Campbellites, Hicksites, New Lights, Universalists and Mormons; and Especially by a Sect Calling Themselves 'Christians'* (1846).

But it hardly ends there.

Less than 1,000 years after Tertullian and Irenaeus, and following a torrent of lesser theological disagreements, disputes, and divisions, the Great Schism of 1054 split Christendom into Eastern and Western Christianity, dominated by various streams of Orthodoxy in the former, by Roman Catholicism in the latter. In the West, little more than a century passed before Pope Lucius III convened the Synod of Verona and promulgated his 1184 bull, *Ab abolendam diversum haeresium pravitatem* (lit., 'To abolish diverse malignant heresies'), which condemned such alternative interpreters of Christianity as the Cathars, the

Waldensians, and the Arnoldists, many of whom advocated an early form of ecclesiastical reform in the Catholic Church. Although not instituting an official inquisition, *Ab abolendam* set the stage for, among other things, the sack of Constantinople in 1204, the Albigensian Crusade against the Cathars in southern France, and the establishment of the Papal Inquisition in 1234 by Pope Gregory IX (see Lambert 1998). Concerned with rooting out heresy wherever it could be found, as the Inquisition grew in ecclesiastical power and geopolitical reach, it investigated such movements as the Spiritual Franciscans, the followers of the early reformer and martyr Jan Hus, and the lay religious Beguines and Beghards (see Lea 1906; Wakefield and Evans 1991). Both the Reformation and Counter-Reformation were grounded in many of the same disputes over what Christianity could and should mean, and those disputes have only increased since. Put differently, 'after one class has discovered some sociological or historical fact', argued Karl Mannheim, 'all other groups, no matter what their interests are, can equally take such fact into account – nay, *must* somehow incorporate such fact into their system of world interpretation' (1952: 147). Sociologically speaking, *all* groups must confront the fact that *any* group sees the world differently than they do, and they must respond in some way.

A Brief Detour in Theory

Since the beginning of the Christian church, believers have demonstrated an astonishing ability to sniff out differences of opinion, and denominational splintering has occurred over everything from Christology and soteriology to dress codes and hymn selection. Theological debates have erupted on topics as varied as voting rights in the congregation, women in the pulpit, and the proper place of poverty in the church, so memorably recounted by Umberto Eco in *The Name of the Rose* (1980). Since no worldview, no framework of existential assumptions and expectations, no *reality* is quite so socially constructed as the religious, all of this happens for one very good reason. That is, as Peter Berger trenchantly reminds us in *The Sacred Canopy*, because 'all socially constructed worlds are inherently precarious' (1967: 29).

Contrary both to popular belief and to the ardent claims of believers, the religious imagination – no matter what form it takes, or what god it serves, or what ritual comfort it provides – is not grounded in certainty. Among other things, if it was, we would not call it faith, our equivocal confidence in 'things we do not see' (Hebrews 11:1). We would not insist that our sacred stories be so regularly ritualized, nor require the constant remembrance of our gods and their commandments, nor cast such a jaundiced eye over those who believe differently than we. That is, when it comes to the supernatural, when it concerns our myriad confusing and often contradictory relationships with what William James called 'the unseen order', forces far more powerful than mere certainty are at work (1902: 61). Chief among these are illusion, fear, and ambivalence. That is, whether a specific act of worship is intended to ensure that the supplicant will be welcomed into the afterlife, whether certain prayers are meant to ensure a good harvest or a set of beliefs is meant to confirm one's membership in the elect, all religious activity rests, among other things, on three pillars: the correlation fallacy, the fear of a false negative, and the power of conviction.

Seeing in one thing the cause of another – whether the two are causally related or not – is the essence of the correlation fallacy. We offer this sacrifice and the harvest is bountiful. We make that ritual atonement and the gods' punishment passes us by. We dutifully repeat a particular set of sacred words – or have them prayerfully repeated on our behalf – and we need no longer fear the endless dark that follows our inevitable death. This illusion of control is the engine of meaning for the religious imagination. It allows us to continue believing that we are active participants in our own destiny, that something we do keeps us secure in the company of the saved. Perhaps most importantly it reinforces the belief that, in the grand scheme of things, we *matter*. Our gods know we are here, and they care about our well-being in some way – so long as we remember and honour them appropriately. No matter how grotesque or benign the rite, or to which species of god it is made, no matter how its priests have dressed it up in the language of ritual and ceremony, every sacrifice ever offered has been made upon this altar (see Cowan 2022: 79–107).

Actively conspiring with this is the fear of a false negative, the deep-seated dread of not paying attention to something when we should, of not doing something when required, of dying unshriven, for instance, for want of a priest on the battlefield. A generation ago, Roman Catholic theologian Ernst Feil argued that prior to the sixteenth century, the dominant mode of the religious imagination in the West was *religio* as opposed to *religion* as we might understand it today. Although at first glance this might seem a distinction without much of a difference, for Feil, "*religio* means the careful and even fearful fulfilment of all that man owes to God or to the gods" (1992: 32). Put differently, this is not the nebulous, metaphysical *something* that so often populates the imaginations of those claiming to be 'spiritual but not religious', but 'something very concrete', 'something very necessary' (Feil 1992: 32). This is the combination of correct doctrinal belief and proper ritual action as if our lives, both here and in the next world, depend on them – because, as far as we are concerned, they do. Indeed, although it is often framed in much more sophisticated theological form, the fear remains the same: a ceremonial misstep, a prayer incorrectly uttered, an unfit sacrifice offered unawares might cast us out from whatever bliss we believe awaits us after death. However layered over it is by tradition and ritual, by ecclesiology and doctrine, this basic anxiety still drives us with a species-wide obsession that positively approaches mania and is central to the Christian countercult mission.

Over time, control of our beliefs and the management of our fears take shape in the form of convictions, which are maintained through cultural convention and reinforced through the comforting presence of fellow believers. This is the well-known externalization-objectivation-internalization arc Berger and Luckmann described in their classic text, *The Social Construction of Reality* (1966). Convictions, especially those with which we are raised and which are constantly repeated for us, help ward off the ambiguity created by the correlation fallacy and the fear of a false negative. That is, while we often hold to our convictions – especially our religious convictions – in spite of contradiction and disproof, in the face of challenge and opposition, their hold on us is always tempered by doubt, by the question scratching unbidden at the edges of our mind even as we sit in our pews: But what if I'm wrong?

Whether provoked by the mutterings of a back-alley Arian insisting that God the Son is not coeternal with God the Father or by the ardent preaching of a new revelation found on golden plates; whether seen in the incipient threat of 'Judaizers' keeping anxious Inquisitors awake at night or the diligence of Matthew Hopkins and his cadre of witch finders scouring the fens and villages of East Anglia; whether it is immigrant Buddhism and Hinduism or the emergence of their syncretized 'New Age' Western variants, the problem is essentially the same: an existential fear that the world as we believe it is and insist that it should be is *not* the world as it actually exists. In that sense, the modern Christian countercult is nothing new. Although the term 'countercult' was not coined until more than a century and a half later, the faith concerns for which modern apologists still contend were on full display by the early part of the nineteenth century, beginning with, though hardly limited to, the nascent Church of Jesus Christ of Latter-day Saints.

Nineteenth-Century Origins of the Christian Countercult

The first edition of the Book of Mormon appeared in 1830. Less than four years later, Eber D. Howe, founder and editor of the *Plainsville Telegraph*, published *Mormonism Unvailed* [*sic*], his nearly 300-page attack on Joseph Smith's nascent church. In good nineteenth-century fashion, Howe laid out much of his case on the title page, which declared that his book represented

> a faithful account of that singular imposition and delusion, from its rise to the present time. With sketches of the characters of its propagators, and a full detail of the manner in which the famous GOLDEN BIBLE was brought

before the world. To which are added inquiries into the probabilities that the historical part of the said Bible was written by one SOLOMON SPAULDING, more than twenty years ago, and by him intended to be sold as a romance. (Howe 1834: n.p., original typography)

Which is to say that Smith and his cohort were not to be trusted, that their religious claims were fraudulent at best, and that much of the Book of Mormon was plagiarized from the unpublished manuscript of an early nineteenth-century novel written by a Congregationalist minister named Solomon Spaulding, a charge that has been levelled throughout the history of hostility to Mormonism. (For LDS replies and counterarguments, see, e.g., Brown and Brown 1981–95; Fluhman 2012; Givens 2013; Scharffs 1989.) Opposite the lengthy title page, the frontispiece to the first edition of Howe's book contains two woodcuts, the upper panel showing Satan gleefully kicking Joseph Smith into the air while the lower depicts Smith preaching to one of his early converts this newfangled doctrine of the devil.

Just a few years after that, Richard Livesey, a Methodist Episcopal minister then preaching in Massachusetts, published *An Exposure of Mormonism, Being a Statement of Facts Relating to the Self-Styled 'Latter-day Saints', and the Origins of the Book of Mormon* (1838). Less the lengthy pamphlet's author than its compiler, Livesey collected the most damning excerpts from other anti-Mormon tracts and letters 'for the purpose of exhibiting in a comprehensive form some important facts concerning the leadership of the Mormon sect, and the origin of the Book of Mormon' (2). In terms of the latter, Livesey recounts a fairly standard encomium of complaints about the Book of Mormon's suspect origin. Having dispensed with that, he assures his readers, 'we next proceed to ·shew what was the principal, if not the only object, in commencing the Mormonite speculation' (6). Which is to say, money. As far as Livesey and his sources were concerned, Joseph Smith was nothing but a grifter playing on people's deepest needs and most deeply ingrained fears. 'Having furnished the above statements', Livesey writes, he 'has only to express his hope that they may be successful in arresting the progress of a delusion which has already occasioned incalculable mischief and which, he is persuaded, has been the ruin of many immortal souls' (12).

Indeed, the decade following the emergence of the LDS church witnessed a plethora of these self-published leaflets, brochures, pamphlets, and books, all drawing upon one another and all making essentially the same claims as Eber Howe. Origen Bacheler's *Mormonism Exposed* even featured the same illustrations as Howe's frontispiece and argued that refuting LDS claims should be considered 'something like a labored attempt to disprove the story of Tom Thumb' (1838: 5). That is, it would not be worth his time, but 'for the fact that some *are* thus duped', and therefore he should be forgiven for 'stooping to notice an affair so intrinsically worthless and contemptible as is the Mormon imposture' (5, 6). Similarly, although Methodist Episcopal minister and abolitionist La Roy Sunderland believed that few 'intelligent people are in much danger of being carried away by a delusion so manifestly monstrous and absurd', if even a handful were 'silly enough to believe the blasphemous absurdities set forth in [The Book of Mormon], we think it is time something more were done to enforce the claims of God's word against such monstrous libels upon truth and religion' (1838: 3; see also, e.g., M'Chesney 1838; Parsons 1841; Winchester 1841).

Like its modern descendant, the embryonic countercult apologetics of the nineteenth century was largely the province of male clerics, lay preachers, and self-appointed apologists, but this is not to say that women took no interest, especially when issues of proper marriage and family were at stake. Between 1880 and 1883, for example, led by firebrand anti-polygamy activist and early Utah suffragist Jennie Anderson Froiseth, the Ladies Anti-Polygamy Society of Utah published a monthly broadsheet, the *Anti-Polygamy Standard*. Aligned with other women's anti-polygamy organizations throughout the United States, as well as groups such the Women's Christian Temperance Union, the eight-page *Standard* not only inveighed against polygamy specifically, but advocated on behalf of women's rights more generally. While the *Standard* kept its subscribers abreast of anti-polygamy activism around the country, it also included advertising that supported its publication, letters to the editor, housekeeping tips, recipes and poems shared by subscribers, and even the occasional humorous clerical anecdote. In keeping with its mandate, however, a significant portion of each issue was devoted to a variety of atrocity stories and commentary designed to highlight what its editor regarded as the worst abuses of the Latter-day Saints.

The ironically titled column 'Beauties of Polygamy' was a regular feature in which LDS women allegedly recounted the horrors of life in their polygamous families, as well as their concurrent fear that were polygamy permitted to continue, it would eventually be forced upon everyone by the LDS Church. Lest anyone question the clear and present danger this prospect represented, Froiseth spread a multipart article across the first few issues outlining the 'Characteristics of Mormon Polygamy', including its inherent 'immorality and licentiousness', how it cannot 'help blunting the moral sense and destroying every vestige of womanly modesty and refinement', and her belief 'that numbers of the men only enter it for the purpose of pandering to their own base passions, and have no religious convictions whatever' (1881: 2). All this opposite 'Housekeeper's Corner', which, among other tips, advised readers that 'grained wood should be washed with cold tea' and that 'cayenne pepper blown into the cracks where ants congregate will drive them away'. Apparently, 'the same remedy is also good for mice' (1881: 2). Above all, wrote 'an editor' (likely Froiseth herself), the *Anti-Polygamy Standard* 'is an appeal for the emancipation of women; it is a protest against that dreadful power which, here in Utah, with the weapons of Superstition and Fear, is beating down the innate and holy instincts of womanhood', indeed 'making her, as nearly as possibly, a mere animal, raised to be at first man's plaything, and later his slave' ('Anti-Polygamy Standard' 1881: 4). Froiseth considered it 'the duty of every wife and mother to aid in circulating the *Anti-Polygamy Standard*'.

When funding for the *Standard* abruptly dried up in 1883 – perhaps because the US Congress' passage of the Edmunds Anti-Polygamy Act of 1882 convinced many of its supporters the battle had been won – Froiseth collected a number of the most salacious anecdotes from the newspaper and republished them as *The Women of Mormonism; or The Story of Polygamy As Told by the Victims Themselves* (1887). Rather than simply point out the horrors of polygamy as she understood them, however, Froiseth also linked the Church of Jesus Christ of Latter-day Saints to an orientalist fear of Islam, one of the most potent nineteenth-century symbols of the mysterious and dangerous religious Other. Claiming that 'Turkey is doubtless the most debased country on earth', she warned everyone within earshot that 'Turkey is in our midst. Modern Mohammedanism has its Mecca at Salt Lake', and 'clearly the Koran was Joseph Smith's model' for 'his foul "revelations"' (Froiseth 1887: xv, xvi). Although many of the nineteenth-century anti-Mormon apologists confined themselves to the LDS Church, Froiseth's specious connection of it to Islam points to a larger issue taking shape as the fin-de-siècle drew near: the dual spectre of increasing religious competition and challenging new scientific ideas.

While 'for climacteric comicality, Mormonism should be awarded the palm', wrote George Hamilton Combs, it was hardly the only 'ism' with which he believed devout Christians should be concerned (1899: 205). Published at the end of the nineteenth century, *Some Latter-day Religions* could be considered one of the first modern compendia of countercult literature. Reminiscent of anti-heresy tracts of the early church, it took vitriolic aim at what the Disciples of Christ minister described as 'the baneful effect of the Athenian itching for new things' abroad in the land (9). Combs also criticized 'Aestheticism', ostensibly the spiritual child of poet Matthew Arnold, but an 'ism' through which 'art was deified, [and] man was degraded' (26). Agnosticism he called 'the apotheosis of ignorance' 'that should be regarded as a soul deformity and a cause for tears' (129, 138). Not unlike Jennie Froiseth's linking of Mormonism and Islam, Combs saw in Theosophy a dangerous eclecticism, a conflation of religious competitors from 'the other side of the sea, Buddhism, Brahmanism, Confucianism', while adding the dangers from 'this side, spiritualism and Christian Science' (33). 'If, after these exposures', he concluded, 'there shall yet be found those who are willing to be duped by this adventuress [i.e., Madame Helena P. Blavatsky], by this out-at-the-elbow eclecticism, by these mild insanities of the Orient, then Puck's motto has been pointed again, "What fools these mortals be"' (47).

Spiritualism he dismissed as 'an unhallowed chorus of lust', convinced that mediums and channelers were 'the leading propagandists of the doctrine of free-love' who 'find justification for illicit love by invoking the spirits of the dead' (185). Likewise, he condemned Christian Science, not so much because of the claims Mary Baker Eddy made in *Science and Health with Key to the Scriptures*, but because 'Christian Science dishonours Christ. It denies His incarnation' (242). More than that, 'it denies His divinity', just as it 'denies reality and efficacy to the suffering of Jesus' (242). Which is to say, it sets aside the principal tenets upon which Combs believed authentic Christianity must inevitably rest in favour of differing theological principles. Throughout *Some Latter-day Religions*, and in defending such cardinal doctrines as the infallibility of Scripture, the Incarnation and full divinity of Jesus, substitutionary atonement, and the reality of the physical resurrection, Combs anticipated by only a few years the spiritual antecedent of the modern Christian countercult, *The Fundamentals*.

'Isms' and *The Fundamentals*

In the first years of the twentieth century, Lyman and Milton Stewart, Southern California oil barons who were identified then only as 'two prominent Christian laymen', underwrote the publication of *The Fundamentals: A Testimony to the Truth*. This was a collection of essays which they maintained established the doctrinal benchmarks and boundaries for acceptable Christian belief and practice. Originally published between 1910 and 1915, *The Fundamentals* appeared first as a series of pamphlets distributed free to 'ministers of the gospel, missionaries, Sunday School superintendents and others engaged in aggressive Christian work throughout the English-speaking world' (Torrey 1917: 5). Rather than the unlettered and unsophisticated devotees so beloved of modern North American cinema and proffered to the world as fundamentalists, however, it is important to remember both that *The Fundamentals* contained essays written by some of the most respected voices in the Christian academy at the time, and that none of the authors would have considered themselves anything other than solidly mainstream in their beliefs. 'Fundamentalism' had not yet acquired the pejorative patina with which it is so often coated today. Indeed, all of the contributors believed nothing other than that they were defending the cardinal and indispensable doctrines of the faith – which is to say, the fundamentals – from a growing motley of tests, trials, and outright threats. The advent of theological liberalism, higher criticism of the Bible, scientific challenges to biblical creationism, and the Darwinian theory of evolution, as well as the so-called New Theology and the Social Gospel, were just some of the problems to which their work was expected to provide an unimpeachable defence.

According to *The Fundamentals*, five essential constituents define the authentic Christian faith: (a) the inerrancy, infallibility, and insuperability of the Bible; (b) the virgin conception of Jesus, his sinless life, crucifixion, and physical resurrection; (c) Jesus' ontological divinity as the Second Person of the Holy Trinity; (d) a substitutionary theory of atonement; and (e) Jesus' literal and visible second coming (see, e.g., Boyer 1992; Marsden 1980; Numbers 1992). Deriving from these, a number of secondary – though no less necessary – elements included belief in original sin and the necessity of personal salvation, a strict moralism that explicitly linked unorthodox belief with inappropriate behaviour, the acceptance of various forms of creationism, and, most important for our purposes, a proactive missionary stance galvanized by literal interpretations of Matthew 28:16–20 and Jude 1:3. Together, these became the benchmarks by which the Christian countercult would evaluate all other faith competitors.

In 1893, the Parliament of the World's Religions brought together for the first time religious practitioners from around the globe to discuss their respective worldviews in a neutral environment. But *The Fundamentals* largely ignored other religions, apart from an essay on 'spiritualism', in which 'the millions of China, Japan and India' are simply dismissed as 'the demonized races of the heathen world' (Pollock 1917: 166). Rather, defence of what the authors came to regard as orthodox Christianity was principally set against deviant Christian sects that had emerged in the nineteenth century, as well as against what many considered the single greatest threat to authentic Christian faith: the Church of Rome. The evangelical Protestant interpretation of Christianity was regarded as self-evidently true and therefore ought to require little more than the refutation of its various challengers to maintain its rightful place in the world.

William Moorehead, for example, then a professor at United Presbyterian Theological Seminary, critiqued Charles Taze Russell's Millennial Dawn movement, the group which became Jehovah's Witnesses. Calling it a 'counterfeit of Christianity', Moorehead criticized both 'Dawnism' and the 'Dawnists' for what he considered their categorical deviance from essential Christian markers, declaring that 'the whole system is anti-Scriptural, anti-Christian, and a deplorable perversion of the Gospel of the Son of God' (1917: 110). Indeed, Moorehead found fault with Russell's interpretation of each of the fundamentals. 'A wretched caricature', he called the Millennial Dawn understanding of the atonement; of the resurrection, it was 'immeasurably worse, if that be possible. Here the climax in audacity and falsehood is reached' (116, 117). As a professor of New Testament literature and exegesis, Moorehead was particularly alarmed by 'the prodigious output of the Watch Tower and Tract Society', highlighting the change in title of Russell's 'six rather bulky volumes' to *Studies in the Scriptures* (109). Moorehead conjectured that the change, and 'the fact that certain evangelical terms are applied to the movement', were intended 'to allay suspicion and to commend the propaganda of Mr. Russell and his followers to the Christian public' (109). Lest this public be deceived, however, Moorehead concludes of 'this vicious system' that 'Millennial Dawn is essentially polytheistic; and as it has always happened with polytheism, this system, should it endure, will ultimately sink into idolatry' (126, 128). While other writers took aim at the Latter-day Saints (McNiece 1917), Christian Science (Wilson 1917), and Spiritualism (Pollock 1917), some recognized that the real threat to evangelical hegemony did not come from Salt Lake City or Boston or even Upstate New York. It came from Rome.

As with other forms of religious antipathy, anti-Catholicism long predates the nineteenth century and has appeared in many forms since well before the Protestant Reformation. From Chaucer's unflattering portrayal of the Monk and the Prioress to Boccaccio's ribald tale of a convent gardener who plays the mute in order to sleep with the nuns; from Denis Diderot's *The Nun* to Matthew Lewis' *The Monk* and the Marquis de Sade's savage portrayals of Roman Catholic clergy in *Juliette, Justine,* and *The 120 Days of Sodom,* what began as caricature and light-hearted satire has traversed a path through pointed social commentary to fetishization and Grand Guignol horror (see Cowan 2022: 108–37).

During the nineteenth century, these fears and anxieties hardened into an anti-Catholic nativism that became something of a cottage industry among North American Protestants distressed at the encroaching power of the Church of Rome, visible in the arrival of waves of immigrants from predominantly Catholic countries. The most well known of these works is the fictitious *Awful Disclosures of Maria Monk* (1836). Putative conventual memoirs such as *The Convent and the Manse* (Hyla 1853) and *Six Months in a Convent* (Reed 1835) were popular reading among those concerned with the challenge presented by Roman Catholicism in general, as well as with those whose more particular prurience turned to the confessional, that yawning portal to the 'lowlands of immorality' (Fresenborg 1904: 86). Atrocity narratives such as *Awful Disclosures* and its sequel, *Further Disclosures of Maria Monk* (1837), were reinforced by anti-Catholic novels such as Helen Dhu's *Stanhope Burleigh,* which was ominously subtitled *Jesuits in our Homes* (1855), and Frances

Trollope's three-volume *Father Eustace: A Tale of the Jesuits* (1847; see Griffin 2004). Nativist newspapers and broadsheets such as *Zion's Herald*, the *New York Evangelist*, and the *New-York Observer and Religious Chronicle* fed the flames of anti-Catholic fervour, a prejudice which many argue continues to this day (Lockwood 2000; Welter 1987). Indeed, perhaps to avoid any confusion as to its journalistic mission, in the late 1830s, *American Protestant Vindicator* changed its name to *American Protestant Vindicator in Defence of Civil and Religious Liberty against the Inroads of Popery*. Later still, it became simply *The Menace*.

Most popular, however, were the kinds of first-person accounts that stirred the Protestant heart and fed its evangelical outrage. Edith O'Gorman, for example, a former nun who taught schoolchildren as Sister Teresa de Chantal, insisted that writing and publishing *Convent Life Unveiled* was motivated solely by her desire to see the truth about Catholicism exposed in the hopes that her story might be the 'means of saving one immortal soul from the slavery of Romanism and the living tomb of convents!' (1871: iv). Former Catholic priest Charles Chiniquy promised readers of *Fifty Years in the Church of Rome* that 'the superstitious, the ridiculous and humiliating practices of the monks, the nuns, and the priests will be shown to you as they were never before' (1886: 5). Indeed, they would 'see the inside life of Popery with the exactness of Photography' (5). Chiniquy's massive tome was a bestseller in Canada, and his earlier work, *The Priest, the Woman, and the Confessional*, went through more than forty printings between its publication in 1880 and the turn of the century. While many contributors to *The Fundamentals* may have turned a jaundiced eye to the gruesome excesses of *Awful Disclosures of Maria Monk* and shaken their heads in dismay over the violent attack on an Ursuline convent in 1834 (see Schultz 2000), this did not mean they dismissed the threat to proper Protestant belief represented by the Vatican.

T. W. Medhurst, for example, who appears to have been a theological student studying under the famous Particular Baptist preacher Charles Haddon Spurgeon, recognized, not unreasonably, that 'if I undertake to prove that *Romanism is not Christian*, I must expect to be called "bigoted, harsh, uncharitable"' (1917: 288; emphasis in the original). This did not dissuade him, however, from declaring that 'the teaching of Rome is at least as different from that of the Sacred Writings as that which Paul calls "another gospel"' (290). Which is to say, the Roman Catholic Church is little more than 'a *Satanic delusion*' (289; emphasis in the original). Reformed Presbyterian pastor J. M. Foster was not willing to take such light-hearted approach. Author also of a self-published pamphlet, 'Romanism, the Evil and Its Remedy', Foster demanded that readers of *The Fundamentals* recognize two 'undeniable facts': 'ROME IS THE NATION'S ANTAGONIST BECAUSE IT IS A CORRUPT

AND CORRUPTING SYSTEM OF FALSEHOOD AND IDOLATRY THAT POLLUTES OUR LAND!' (1917: 301; emphasis in the original). As if that was not sufficiently clear, he declares the Vatican a threat to the Republic as well as to the one true Church: 'ROME IS THE NATION'S ANTAGONIST BECAUSE IT IS A POLITICAL SYSTEM OF FOREIGN DESPOTISM!' (309; emphasis in the original). Indeed, Foster's Protestant nativism was already crystal clear when he wrote two decades earlier that, notwithstanding the First Amendment's Free Exercise Clause, 'it is the State's duty to suppress all open idolatry, whether it be in the endowment-house of the Mormons, the Joss-houses of the Chinamen, or the Roman Catholic Cathedral; it is the Church's privilege to enforce the worship of the true God within her pale. It belongs to the State to punish blasphemy' (Foster 1894: 11).

And for those who feared the decline and fall of the evangelical Christian empire, there was plenty of blasphemy to punish and worship of the one true God to enforce.

2 The Modern Countercult Movement in North America

All this is not to say that there were no moderate voices trying to find a hearing in the face of widespread distribution of *The Fundamentals*. Both Gaius Glenn Atkins and Charles Samuel Braden, for example, discuss many of the same groups castigated by these other writers, but do so in a much more thoughtful and circumspect manner. In *Modern Religious Cults and Movements*, Atkins, a Congregationalist minister and professor of homiletics at Auburn Seminary, pointed out that human understanding of the Divine could hardly be considered a fixed point in theological space, contained there as something immutable and eternal. Rather, our relationship with the unseen order, however we understand it, 'must be plastic and changing', evolving even as we ourselves evolve (1923: 339). And even though his book was brought out by same prominent evangelical press that had published both Charles Chiniquy and George Hamilton Combs, Atkins argued that emergent and alternative religious movements were, in fact, real-world examples of precisely that plasticity and evolution, and he commended them as 'aspects of the creative religious consciousness of the age' (338).

Similarly, in *These Also Believe*, Charles Samuel Braden suggested that 'by the term "cult" I mean nothing derogatory to any group so classified. A cult, as I define it, is any religious group which differs significantly in some one or more respects as to belief or practice from those religious groups which are regarded as the normative expressions of religion in our total culture' (1949: xii). His use of 'cult' notwithstanding, Braden, who taught religious studies at Northwestern

University for nearly thirty years, proposed a sociological understanding of the issue, rather than one lodged in theological difference understood as schismatic deviance. That is, deviance is best understood as a function of social difference, not as an evaluation of religious validity (see, e.g., Stark and Bainbridge 1985, 1997). Indeed, Braden continued, 'if any reader belongs to a group discussed here prefers to think of himself as a member of a minority religious group rather than a cult, there can be no objection' (1949: xii). Which is to say, these also believe and should not be denigrated or dismissed merely for believing differently. Others, however, were not nearly so sanguine.

Within the Christian Reformed Church, Jan Karel van Baalen is remembered principally for his contribution to the 'common grace' controversy that took place in that denomination during the 1920s. Arguing on the side of so-called common grace, van Baalen believed that the grace of God is at least implicit in all humanity, as opposed to those who contended that God's 'special grace' is available only to the elect. Irving Hexham and Karla Poewe point out that this more expansive theological position led to his 'effort to be scrupulously fair' when it came to his writings on new religious movements, most notably *The Chaos of Cults*, first published in 1938. That is, van Baalen's 'objections were doctrinal, not personal or vindictive' (1997: 3). This is not to say, though, that he was not as deeply concerned about the advent of new and alternative religions as those whose criticisms of them were more trenchant and less temperate.

In the introduction to *Chaos*' last edition, van Baalen celebrated the fact that the previous decades had seen 'a vast increase in the study and disapproval of the anti-Christian cults' (van Baalen 1960: 6), but he warned that the 'negative approach to the cults' by which so much of the nineteenth century had been characterized 'would never suffice' (6). When confronting the adherent of a different faith, for example, he advised that one should 'never show that you suspect the cultist of dishonesty or mercenary motives' (392). In direct contrast to much of what has followed in the Christian countercult, new religious believers should be approached as though the *motives* behind their faith choices were as authentic and honourable as anyone else's. For van Baalen, this was not simply tactics, but a direct expression of his belief in common grace. Even in groups he considered particularly odious – Jehovah's Witnesses, for example, he called 'the deadliest and most fierce enemies of the Christian religion today' (266) – he believed that 'there is a sufficient amount of common grace working in most men for them to resent being suspected of evil' (393).

Although van Baalen does seem to be calling for a 'kinder, gentler' apologetics than was seen in many of his predecessors and contemporaries, he still laments an unfortunate 'increase in tolerance towards' these 'anti-Christian cults' (6). He points, for example, to a well-known feature of small towns across North

America: the municipal signboard advertising local religious congregations, service groups, and fraternal organizations. While, for most of their history, these listings might have been limited to culturally acceptable faith traditions – St. Paul's Methodist, St. Mary's Catholic Church, almost certainly Grace Christian Reformed – more recently, the problem was that 'Mormonism, Christian Science, Unity, and similar non-Christian cults are allowed to list their services and hours of worship on the same bulletin boards at the entrance of cities and towns, and in hotel lobbies, with evangelical churches whose every tenet these cults not merely deny but combat' (6). Lest the reader be left in any doubt, van Baalen concludes that 'the writer believes that it would be well to stop this practice' (6).

Although it resembles such works as Combs' *Some Latter-day Religions* and William C. Irvine's *Heresies Exposed* (1935), *The Chaos of Cults* represents a watershed moment in the formation of the modern Christian countercult. Subtitled *A Study in Present-day Isms*, it was one of the first books to treat emergent religions in systematic fashion, cutting through the chaos, as it were. That is, rather than relying solely on antipathetic bombast and theological outrage, van Baalen attempted to understand why adherents of new religions believed the way they did. Each chapter presents a brief history of a particular group, an explanation of its doctrines and theologies, as well as selections from its own writings and prophets. As far as he was able, van Baalen tried to understand these 'present-day isms' in their own contexts. This did not prevent him, however, from thoroughly salting his work with disdain for these alternative spiritual paths. Baha'i temples, for example, are marked by 'frightfully outlandish names', while Mormon polygamy is the natural result of 'the hankering after sexual indulgence that characterized' the founders of the LDS church (159, 215). While he admits that 'there is much in [Seventh-day Adventism] that is praiseworthy', he still declares that the entire enterprise 'goes far beyond the limits of sound and sober sense' (257, 259). To reinforce these perceptions, each chapter concludes with a section entitled 'Aids to Study' which were likely designed for use in an adult Sunday School classroom. 'Is Baha'ism as tolerant as it pretends to be?' he asks at one point, and 'Where lies the origin of the entire Adventist error?' at another (170, 265). Possibly my favourite, however, is a thought experiment that reads: 'A minister has a suite of rooms for rent. Two men rang his doorbell and said, "We are Christians. We'd like to rent your rooms." He discovered they were "Latter-day Saints", and refused them, citing II John 10. Was the minister right?' (236). For the record, 2 John 10:10 reads: 'If there come any unto you, and bring not this doctrine, receive him not into your house, neither bid him God speed.'

Van Baalen's encyclopedic approach laid the foundation for much of the countercult work that has followed, and was clearly a major precursor to Walter Martin's *Kingdom of the Cults*, as well as numerous other countercult digests. Van

Baalen's almost throwaway concluding comment – that 'the cults are the unpaid bills of the church' (420) – has become an axiomatic battle cry for countercult apologetics, appearing in everything from seminary courses to blog posts, and from the introduction to Martin's *magnum opus* to advertising for the C. S. Lewis Institute. However, like George Hamilton Combs, who was known as the 'millionaire preacher' at Kansas City's Independence Boulevard Christian Church, and William C. Irvine, who spent his career as a missionary and superintendent of the Belgaum Leprosy Hospital in the Western ghats region of India, van Baalen's countercult activity was always adjunct to his principal calling as a pastor and Christian Reformed intellectual. He believed firmly, though, that any new religion represented an existential threat to the only real faith in which humankind should place its trust. For him, there could be no ecumenical 'agree-to-disagree' meeting of religions. 'Not only has the cultist repudiated the orthodox religion you represent', he wrote to those who sought to take the fight beyond their pews and confront 'adherents of the cults' directly, 'he is actually hostile to it ... The cultist you are about to visit is your *opponent* (389, 391; emphasis in the original). Thus, 'you should be able to attack and refute his stand. Refute his principle, the foundation of his system' (395). Bluntly, van Baalen advised his readers: 'Destroy the foundation, and the excrescences will disappear' (396). This became the sine qua non of Christian countercult apologetics, and what shifted the balance from avocational apologetics to a modern apologetics movement.

Modern Countercult Apologetics

In theological terms, apologetics has been defined as 'the defence of the Christian faith on intellectual grounds by trained theologians and philosophers' (Cross and Livingstone 1983: 73). By the end of the second century, apologists had become concerned with explaining and defending what they regarded as the truths of the Christian faith, whether to other Christians or to adherents of competing religions, such as Judaism. According to Frank Cross and Elizabeth Livingstone, the practice of apologetics was understood as the means by which (a) religious belief in general is presented as more rational than non-belief, and (b) that the Christian faith in particular is the most rational choice from all available options (73). Echoing van Baalen, Kenneth Boa and Robert Bowman argue that, in the context of the evangelical Christian church, this has developed to mean 'a *defense* of Christianity as a system, a *vindication* of the Christian worldview against its assailants, and a *refutation* of opposing systems and theories' (Boa and Bowman 2001: 20). Or, put more precisely, at least as far as members of the countercult are concerned, vindication *by means of* refutation, as though the latter necessarily entails the former.

What began with books such as *The Chaos of Cults* and *Kingdom of the Cults* now consists of everything from full-service apologetics organizations such as the CRI to church-run apologetics and outreach ministries. Coalitions such as EMNR bring together groups that may only focus on one or two new religious movements (e.g., Saints Alive in Jesus). Countercult material is now regularly offered in courses at evangelical seminaries and Bible colleges and replicated on a plethora of rudimentary websites, blogs, and YouTube channels. Whether they identify as apologetics think tanks, discernment ministries, or resource clearinghouses, the organizational structure of the Christian countercult can be parsed along a number of continua.

One axis, for instance, might plot the spectrum in terms of a group's relative professionalization. That is, how much of what it does has become a professional pursuit for those involved, as opposed to an avocation? The CRI, which Walter Martin founded in 1960, has established itself as one of the first professional countercult apologetics organizations. Through the *Bible Answer Man* call-in radio programme and the monthly *Christian Research Journal*, as well as a variety of multimedia podcasts, videos, and dedicated online material, it remains one of the most prominent. Although the online history still erroneously describes Martin as 'the first Christian evangelical clergy to recognize the threat and opportunity presented to the Church by cults and alternative religious systems', the CRI claims to be 'the largest and most effective apologetics ministry in the world' ('Our History' 2022). While this latter claim is debatable, the effect of the CRI on the apologetics landscape and the model it provided for other similar ministries is undeniable. Through both its imitators and emulators in the CCM, as well as the many former employees and researchers who have struck out on their own, the influence of Martin's CRI continues to be felt throughout the wider apologetics domain.

The Institute for Religious Research (IRR), for example, is helmed by Rob Bowman, a former CRI researcher. Focusing mainly on Jehovah's Witnesses and the Church of Jesus Christ of Latter-day Saints, the IRR offers a range of resources on various topics related to evangelical apologetics. Profiles on these as well as other religious groups – Zen Buddhism, Islam, and Roman Catholicism, to name a few – are provided courtesy of WF. Founded in 1979 by David Henke, a teacher who chose to leave that profession for full-time apologetics, WF is now managed by James K. Walker, a former Latter-day Saint. Describing itself as 'a counter-cult and watchdog ministry', WF offers four-day 'cult awareness conferences', as well as an 'Area-Wide Cult Impact Conference' 'designed to impact the entire community' ('Mission Statement' n. d.; 'Programs & Presentations' n.d.). On 'Cult Awareness Sundays', a WF staffer visits a local congregation and presents an abbreviated version of these longer programmes, including 'adult Sunday school classes for an overview of the cults, a morning sermon on the cults and an evening service designed to introduce Mormonism, Jehovah's Witnesses and/or the New Age Movement' ('Programs & Presentations' n.d.). Watchman Fellowship's bread-and-butter resource, however, comprises the four-to-five-page profiles it has produced bimonthly for nearly twenty years (e.g., Branch 1994). Encouraging members and site visitors 'to begin their own religious research notebooks', these profiles have recently been collected into the 600-page *Watchman Fellowship Profile Notebook*.

The Centers for Apologetics Research (CFAR) follows a different axis, serving as the hub for a group of 'international countercult ministries'. It describes its mission as 'equipping God's people across borders and cultures for discernment, defense of the faith and cult evangelism' ('About CFAR' 2022). Founded by Paul Carden, another CRI alumnus who worked closely with Walter Martin for fifteen years, CFAR's goals are threefold: (a) 'to warn God's people' about the dangers represented by 'the cults, occult, and aberrant Christian believers'; (b) 'to train' these believers 'to discern between truth and error and defend the faith'; and (c) 'to mobilize' in an effort 'to resist the advance of the cults and win cultists to Jesus Christ' ('About CFAR' 2022).

Although headquartered in the United States, CFAR builds on Carden's experience as a countercult missionary in Brazil and focuses on apologetics in the international context, specifically its mission 'to equip Christians in the developing world' ('About CFAR' 2022). To that end, it maintains 'affiliate ministries' in Russia and Hungary, two separate organizations in Brazil, and one serving the rest of Latin America. 'Frontier Ministries' include the 'Africa Centre for Apologetics Research' (A/CFAR), which covers Uganda, Kenya, Tanzania, Rwanda, and Burundi, as well as 'the rest of English-speaking Africa' and 'the rest of sub-Saharan Africa' ('About CFAR' 2022). Among the groups A/CFAR considers either cults or controversial are: Ahmadiyya Muslims, Baha'i, and Seventh-day Adventists. Finally, CFAR has established 'partnership ministries' in Ethiopia, the Philippines, and Romania. The latter, for example, describes itself as 'an online body of materials to help build up the body of Christ', most of which are translated articles originally published by various alumna of the CRI ('About Us' 2022). The fine print at the bottom of each of CFAR's website pages states 'that the inclusion of materials about a particular group ... does not necessarily mean that the group is considered a destructive cult' – an important point to which we will return. Despite this disclaimer, visitors are encouraged to subscribe to regular 'ministry updates' and to check the box marked, '**Yes!** I would also like to receive: **Cultic Trend Alert**' ('Updates' 2022; emphasis in the original).

Yet a different trajectory is taken by organizations that limit their apologetic efforts to specific groups, often those of which the founders were members. Ed Decker, for example, co-author of *The Godmakers*, was a Latter-day Saint for twenty years before leaving the church and shortly thereafter founding his countercult ministry, Saints Alive in Jesus. Jerald and Sandra Tanner were both raised in the LDS church, but converted to evangelical Christianity as adults. Since 1983, they have operated Utah Lighthouse Ministry and Bookstore from a small, neat bungalow located barely two kilometres from Temple Square in Salt Lake City. Although not raised as a Latter-day Saint, Bill McKeever founded Mormonism Research Ministry in 1979 'as a missionary/apologetics organization' that not only provides a variety of print and online resources, but also 'takes the gospel directly to the Mormon people by conducting outreach at Mormon events such as temple openings and pageants' ('What We Do' n.d.).

While each of these various ministries – and the many dozens of others which could have been included in this Element – share a similar worldview, perhaps the most useful way of understanding the Christian countercult is actually by distinguishing it from its non-religious counterpart, the secular ACM.

3 Telling the Christian Countercult from the Secular Anticult

In 1993, Italian scholar Massimo Introvigne proposed a rationalist/post-rationalist quadrilateral to explain the differences between secular and faith-based opposition to new religious movements (NRMs). On the one hand, for the *secular anticult*, rationalist opposition was marked by its perception of 'religious opportunism' (e.g., NRM leaders looking to fleece their flock), while *Christian countercult* apologists regarded new religious competitors as spiritual frauds, poisoned fruit of the satanic tree. On the other hand, *post*-rationalist reasoning, argued Introvigne, was grounded in the former's commitment to the brainwashing hypothesis, while the latter demonized their religious opponents as enemies with whom they are engaged in 'spiritual warfare' that has been ongoing since the Edenic fall (Introvigne 1995: 36; see also Introvigne 1993, 2022b).

Psychologist Michael D. Langone disagreed, criticizing Introvigne's distinction as both 'an oversimplification and subtly derogatory' (1995: 171). At the time, Langone was serving as the executive director of the American Family Foundation (now the International Cultic Studies Association, or ICSA) and editor of its then-flagship publication, *Cultic Studies Journal*. Arguing that the two countermovements – secular and faith-based – represented 'complementary visions, not irresolvable conflicts', Langone objected that Introvigne's model 'leads to a construction or exaggeration of differences, as well as an underestimation of similarities' (172–3). That is, as far as he was concerned, Introvigne had seriously misunderstood the secular anticult position, and sociologists and psychologists researching new religious movements should engage in more productive, which is to say mutually supportive, dialogue (see Almendros et al. 2013).

Although little has changed in the basic accuracy of Introvigne's assessment, for the decades both prior to it and since, academic interest in anti-NRM countermovements has focused mainly on the secular anticult. This has been motivated primarily by the anticult's high-profile reliance on the brainwashing hypothesis as an explanation for new religious conversion and retention, as well as its controversial and, in many cases, illegal practice of forcible deprogramming and coercive exit counselling (see, e.g., Barker 1984; Bromley and Richardson 1983; Bromley and Shupe 1981, 1987; Shupe and Bromley 1980, 1995; Shupe, Bromley, and Oliver 1984; Shupe, Spielmann, and Stigall 1977).

Acknowledging that religiously oriented countermovements were not limited to evangelical Christianity, Introvigne concluded nevertheless that the differences between secular and faith-based movements were sufficiently significant that conflict between them was not only all but inevitable, but should be explored in more depth. Setting any 'apparent similarities aside', I noted nearly a decade later, 'there *are* significant enough differences between the ACM and the CCM – e.g., in their respective cult conceptualizations, epistemologies, threat perceptions, and organizational motivation and methods – that some further distinction between the two movements is in order' (Cowan 2002: 340). That is, while they may share a level of general concern about new, alternative, or controversial religious groups, the two movements are simply not the same. Among other things, extraction and exit constitute the order of the day for the secular anticult, while successful apologetics will always result in conversion for the countercult. This hope for a migration away from any and all forms of 'false religion' and into the bosom of the one true faith constitutes a major difference.

Conceptualization: Defining the Dangerous Cult

As we saw in Section 1, faith-based opposition to new competitors in the religion marketplace has existed far longer than that of their secular counterparts. The fact that more people today rely on anticult representations of the problem, however, should not come as a surprise. Exorcisms may constitute a significant part of particular Christian subcultures, but their appearance in popular culture is limited almost exclusively to horror cinema and quasi-documentaries stocked as Halloween fare by Internet streaming services (e.g., Larson 1999, 2016; Larson and Larson 2017; cf. Cowan 2003a: 79–95; 2008: 167–200). In contrast, the spectre of brainwashing and its counterparts, forcible deprogramming and the equally objectionable 'exit counselling', show up with alarming regularity in pop culture products ranging from crime dramas and forensic or legal procedurals to situation comedy and so-called infotainment programming.

For many years and in a number of different undergraduate courses, I have used what I call my 'Dangerous Cult Exercise', the object of which is not so much to spell out for students what constitutes a 'dangerous cult', but to engage in a thought experiment intended to confront them with the fundamental difficulties of the task. Working in groups, students 'must arrive at consensus on the following three questions: (a) How should we define a "dangerous cult"? What indicators should we use in our assessment of religious groups? (b) What obligations do we have to the wider society? How should we weigh civil liberties and social harmony in the balance? And (c) what are your recommendations? That is, what measures, if any, should we implement in response to this issue?' (Cowan forthcoming). Having run the exercise many times, and even though the vast majority of students are encountering this kind of material for the first time, the various criteria they generate almost exclusively mirror those proposed by the secular anticult – for example, a charismatic leader to whom members must swear allegiance and obedience; reliance on brainwashing to recruit and retain members; an alarming level of secrecy, particularly when it comes to group finances; sexual predation by group leaders; and, arguably the most common, a propensity, or at least the potential, for violence, whether internally or externally directed.

Although none of the students have ever heard of prominent anticult figures such as Margaret Singer or Michael Langone, attributes of the secular anticult definition on which they rely have permeated popular culture to the extent that these are virtually the only concepts available to students in terms of addressing the questions in the exercise. 'Put plainly', I note elsewhere, and 'despite the best efforts and fondest delusions of the academy, far more people learn about new religious movements – whether labelled "cults" or not – from popular culture than they do from reputable scholarship or university coursework' (Cowan forthcoming). From brainwashing and thought control to religious hucksterism and sexual assault, from the appearance of mindless religious zombies to apocalyptically dangerous zealots, these various tropes supply the cultural stock of knowledge about unfamiliar religious movements of all kinds, whether a specific criterion applies or not. Pop culture representations become their 'recipe knowledge' – 'the sum total of "what everybody knows"' – on which they rely, in this case, to evaluate new, alternative, and possibly controversial religious movements (Berger and Luckmann 1966: 83; see Cowan 2008: 201–48).

And that's the problem.

The ICSA, which remains the only large-scale North American anticult organization to survive the twentieth century, developed a list of 'characteristics associated with cultic groups' that has grown over the years. Special pleading and lengthy disclaimers notwithstanding, the list has become no more precise and no less problematic than when it was when first proposed (see Langone 2015a, 2015b). Although Langone insists that 'this list is not meant to be a "cult scale" or definitive checklist' (Langone 2015a), it is difficult to understand how those who are already disposed to see the worst in new religious conversion and affiliation, those who make their living, in whole or in part, by identifying suspect groups and counselling those involved, or those who are searching for some way to explain the disturbing new religious behaviour of their friends and loved ones could view its criteria differently. Indeed, implicitly invoking the brainwashing hypothesis, Langone warns that 'many members, former members, and supporters of cults' – that is, historians, psychologists, and sociologists of religion (including the author of this Element) who have opposed the secular anticult's activities and been labelled 'cult apologists' for their trouble – 'are not fully aware of the extent to which members may have been manipulated, exploited, even abused' (Langone 2015a). In a less-than-subtle ad hominem, and in a way that echoes Christian countercult rhetoric about its own critics, if someone does not support the anticult position, they are either ill informed about NRMs in general or potentially in collusion with suspect religious groups. That is, if you don't agree with us, you are either ignorant of the issue or part of the problem.

Among the fifteen characteristics which may (or may not) apply, the ICSA cites as potential 'cause for concern' the following: that a 'group is elitist, claiming a special, exalted status for itself', and 'has a polarized us-versus-them mentality'; that the group 'is preoccupied with bringing in new members' and particularly 'with making money'; and that 'members are expected to devote inordinate amounts of time to the group and group-related activities' and display 'excessively zealous and unquestioning commitment to its leader'. More than that, among these members, 'questioning, doubt, and dissent are discouraged or even punished', while 'mind-altering practices (such as meditation, chanting, speaking in tongues, denunciation sessions, and debilitating work routines) are used in excess', most often as a means of ensuring compliance among members (Langone 2015a). To accompany the ICSA's latest cultic inventory, Langone published an article purportedly addressing long-standing concerns about the list's internal ambiguity and the clear potential for abuse it presents (2015b).

It is difficult to know just where to begin with such a hodge-podge of anxiety and concern. Notwithstanding the constant use of provisional and contingent language, how could any of these so-called characteristics be measured in an empirically reliable way, or in a manner that could be responsibly applied to an entire religious group? How, for example, does one determine an appropriate level of zeal, as opposed to one that is excessive? It is all but axiomatic that what seems onerous to one person may not even show up on another's perceptual radar. On the other hand, what groups are not in some way 'preoccupied' with bringing in new members, especially groups concerned with addressing specific social and/or religious problems? And what about groups which show no interest in recruitment and are quite content to remain small and insular, but which might meet some of the other criteria? What constitutes an 'excess' of meditation or chanting or speaking in tongues – all of which, it needs to be said, are well-known devotional practices in any number of religious traditions around the world? Similarly, is there an appropriate level of 'debilitating work', and who decides what constitutes an 'inordinate amount of time' spent in group activities?

And these are not the only questions raised by the ICSA conceptualization of new religions. How many of these putative characteristics must be present and to what degree in order for a group to be declared dangerous or abusive? Moreover – and this cannot be overstated – who makes those determinations and on what grounds? Since the majority of testimony relied upon by the secular anticult comes from former members, many of whom left their respective groups under strained circumstances and may be seeking either vindication or retribution, how does the ICSA propose to measure the veracity of anecdotal atrocities against the experiences of current members who are happy, healthy, and quite prepared to continue their affiliation? How does the ICSA assess the testimony from aggrieved family members and friends? Despite its disclaimers, the ICSA still seems not to have recognized in the least the fact that these are all highly personal and idiosyncratic variables open to profound countermovement abuse.

Though there is little indication that the anticult's position has changed, one of the major problems in this regard remains the inability to distinguish between groups which share these characteristics, but which the ICSA does *not* consider dangerous or abusive. Arguably, this is the single most problematic issue with the anticult conceptualization of the dangerous cult. Indeed, for many years, when called upon to serve as expert witnesses in NRM-related court proceedings, Margaret Singer and her colleagues felt compelled to bring a series of talking points to answer the question of 'Aren't the Marines a cult by your definition?' Obviously, these points were intended to highlight salient differences, but the very fact that the ICSA has had to clarify this with such regularity demonstrates the fundamentally ambiguous nature – and corresponding unreliability – of its definition (see Cowan 2002; Singer and Lalich 1995: 98–101). Yet nearly half a century on from the cult panics of the 1970s and 1980s, and despite the numerous other problems inherent in the anticults' approach, this precise argument still circulates both in anticult discourse and in the research materials anticults provide to the public.

In 2013, seeking some form of rapprochement between the secular anticult and its academic critics, the directors of the ICSA published an open letter in which they noted that 'although cultic groups vary a great deal, a huge body of clinical evidence and a growing body of empirical research indicate that *some groups harm some people sometimes*, and that some groups may be more likely to harm people than other groups' (Almendros et al. 2013; emphasis added). The rub here is that this has never been in dispute. Ever. Some groups do harm some people sometimes, occasionally with a shocking level of violence. The problem remains, though, that – the open letter's shockingly naïve conclusion notwithstanding – the secular anticult continues to rely on a highly unstable labelling mechanism to identify these groups in a post hoc fashion, but then to generalize from them propter hoc. Even nearly three decades on, this approach seems more suited to the political evaluation and personal condemnation of unpopular religious choices than the dispassionate analysis of potential harm that it purports to be.

Fortunately, no such ambiguity obtains for the Christian countercult. Indeed, quite the opposite. While some countercult apologists offer an occasional, grudging nod to issues of thought control and deceptive recruiting, restrictive jurisdiction over members, or the suspect power of group leadership, these rank a distant and indistinct second to the *ur*-principle guiding their apologetics: the ongoing need to confront theological deviance wherever it is found and in whatever form. That is, all religious competitors are evaluated in terms of normative claims to the uniqueness and insuperability of evangelical Christianity as the apologists themselves understand it. Thus, writes Walter Martin in the mid-1950s, '*by cultism we mean the adherence to doctrines which are pointedly contradictory to orthodox Christianity* . . . in short, any major deviation from orthodox Christianity relative to the cardinal doctrines of the Christian faith' (1955: 12; emphasis in the original). The majority of countercult writings addressed concerns related to this point exactly, namely alternative interpretations of the Christian message, especially those that emerged in the nineteenth century: Christian Science, the Church of Jesus Christ of Latter-day Saints, and Jehovah's Witnesses, to name only the most prominent. In the years that followed, however, as the North American religion marketplace expanded further, Martin devoted numerous *Bible Answer Man* broadcasts, public talks, and recorded Bible studies based on his *Kingdom of the Cults* to the conviction that all religions other than his particular version of Christianity were suspect at best, fraught with peril at worst.

Other countercult apologists, however, explicitly reject the brainwashing hypothesis, recognizing not only that it is both too subjective and prone to its own abuse, but also that it avoids what they consider the real issue. Gretchen Passantino (d. 2014), for example, who founded Answers in Action with her husband, Bob (d. 2003), both of whom worked as staff researchers at Martin's CRI, maintained that '*doctrinal* aberration should distinguish cults from Christianity, not merely social aberration' (G. Passantino 1997: 55; emphasis in the original). For the Passantinos, who, despite their own views and close association with Martin, criticized the lengths to which some apologists went in their pursuit of theological things that go bump in the night (1990b; see also Spencer 1993), a cult was defined as 'a religious group that identifies itself with Christianity, or at least claims compatibility with Christianity, and yet denies one or more of its cardinal biblical doctrines' (Passantino and Passantino 1990a). Like Martin, however, a review of the groups included in the Passantinos' list of suspect groups demonstrates that any world religion, faith tradition, NRM, or spiritual enterprise that deviates from these 'cardinal biblical doctrines' should be considered a cult, if only by implication.

Moreover, writes Bob Larson in his eponymous *New Book of Cults*, 'the term *cult* is generally understood to have a negative connotation that indicates morally reprehensible practices or beliefs that depart from historic Christianity' (1989: 19). That is, any group that 'ignores or purposely omits central apostolic doctrines' or 'holds beliefs that are distinctly opposed to orthodox Christianity' is to be considered a cult (19, 20). Never mind that throughout the history of the Christian church, morally reprehensible practices have often been conducted precisely on the grounds of these central apostolic doctrines. The evangelical sociologist Ronald Enroth, whose particular concern is young people and NRMs, agrees with Larson, but makes his case even more starkly. Writing in *The Lure of the Cults*, Enroth declares that 'any group, movement, or teaching may be considered cultic to the degree it deviates from biblical, orthodox Christianity' (1979: 20; see also, e.g., Ankerberg and Weldon 1991, 1999; Hanegraff 2009; Howard, Fink, and Unseth 1990; McDowell and Stewart 1983; Scott 1993; Williams 1997).

As countercult apologetics grew in popularity among evangelicals and came to define in more oppositional ways the essential differences between their beliefs and virtually any other, the range of groups with which evangelicals expressed explicit concern expanded dramatically. The Evangelical Ministries to New Religions, for example, a coalition of Christian countercult groups founded in 1982, changed its name in 2022 to Evangelical Ministries to Non-Christian Religions, a not-unimportant shift. Although some apologists still seek to distinguish between cults – which they consider theological deviations by those claiming to be Christian – from the orthodox teachings of the historic Christian faith and false religions – interpreted as *any* divergence from Christian belief whatsoever – in practice this is a distinction without much of a difference. Thus, Ron Rhodes is as likely to publish *Reasoning from the Scriptures with Mormons* (1995) as he is *Reasoning from the Scriptures with Muslims* (2002) or *Reasoning from the Scriptures with Catholics* (2000). Bob Larson is as likely to denounce the so-called demonic in Hinduism (1969) as he is in 'Satanic folk religions' such as 'Voodoo, Santeria and Macumba' (1999: 171–83). And Zondervan's Guide to Cults and Religious Movements series is as likely to include entries on *'Jesus Only' Churches* and *Jehovah's Witnesses* (Beisner 1998; Bowman 1994) as it is *Astrology and Psychic Phenomena, Unitarian Universalism,* and *Buddhism, Taoism and Other Far Eastern Religions* (Holley and Kole 1996; Gomes 1998b; Yamamoto 1998, respectively). Even the Passantinos' operating definition of a cult did not prevent them from authoring the Zondervan apologetics guide to *Satanism* (1995), or from advising parents anxious about the occasional satanic panic what to do *When the Devil Dares Your Kids* (1991).

For the Christian countercult, these are all of a piece and all equally dangerous.

Theory: Explaining 'Cultic Behaviour'

Before considering the specific theories on which either the secular anticult or the Christian countercult bases its opposition to so-called cultic behaviour, it is important to understand what theory is and what it is meant to do, if for no other reason than that the concept is so often misunderstood or misapplied. Put simply and, in my view, most usefully, a theory can be defined as a systematic explanation for a particular set of observed facts. That is, *a theory explains something*, whether we find credence in the evidence on which it is based or not, accept or reject the arguments as presented, and, in the end, agree or disagree with the explanation. In terms of opposition to religious groups which either the anticult or the countercult considers problematic, then, because a theory offers nothing more or less than a proposed explanation for something, the issue of validity – of whether this or that theory is actually true – is often not so much moot as beside the point. More significant are questions of how particular theories emerge and develop, what purposes they serve in specific contexts and among different constituencies, how well they account for conflicting data and integrate outlier cases, and how they survive or change in the face of alternative explanations for the same set of observed facts. At this level, we are interested in how they map the differing sociologies of knowledge according to which diverse cultural groups understand and navigate the world. Like the definitions deployed by the secular anticult and the Christian countercult, the frameworks of explanation offered by each for the emergence and resilience of controversial religious movements are also very different.

For the secular anticult, the underpinning explanatory logic is a straightforward syllogism: (a) no one in full possession of their faculties, who is (b) presented with all the relevant facts and given ample opportunity to make their own decisions, (c) would choose to join a new or controversial religious movement; therefore, (d) for those who appear to have made this choice, these faculties and processes must have been impaired, constrained, or controlled in some way. That is, since no one would willingly become a cult member, something else must be at work. *Res ipsa loquitur.* In this way, though now softened somewhat as 'thought control' or 'thought reform', the brainwashing hypothesis describes an almost perfect tautological circle deriving from many of the so-called characteristics by which the anticult defines potentially dangerous religious groups. Indeed, it provides a full-service theory, explaining in equal measure recruitment, affiliation, resistance to exit, even recidivism on the part of group members. Mind-altering practices and debilitating work routines, indoctrination sessions which reinforce perceptions of an elitist or special, exalted status, even the amount of time devoted to the group and group-related activities, including meditation, chanting, and denunciation sessions – all can be fashioned into support for a brainwashing explanation.

Consider the ideological value of such a theory. It rationalizes the most egregious interpretations of suspect religious groups and thereby justifies whatever action the anticult actors feel necessary, all the while offering a palatable explanation to distressed parents and concerned friends for the aberrant religious behaviour of their loved ones. As David Bromley and I point out, the brainwashing hypothesis supplied the ACM with its three principal conceptual supports: (a) it 'effectively obviated claims made by new religion adherents that their conversions were voluntary and genuine'; (b) it 'summarily removed responsibility for conversion from the individual and placed it squarely in the domain of "devious cult leaders"'; and (c), of perhaps most concern in terms of coercive deprogramming (i.e., kidnapping and unlawful confinement), it 'laid the conceptual foundation for parents' legal custody over their adult children by having them declared incompetent' (Cowan and Bromley 2015: 94; see Bromley and Richardson 1983; Cowan and Bromley 2015: 78–98).

Even more than that, brainwashing 'became a kind of cultural mythology, an overarching explanatory framework both for the explosive emergence of new religious movements toward the end of the 1960s and for the alleged success these groups had in recruiting members' (Cowan and Bromley 2015: 94). And, as my own 'Dangerous Cult Exercise' seems to demonstrate, despite lack of any empirical support for the validity of brainwashing as a process, as well as its stunning lack of success in groups most often accused of employing it, brainwashing remains among the most common pop culture tropes used to describe and demonize NRMs. Although billed as a romantic comedy, for example, one of the most disturbing portrayals of the brainwashing–deprogramming dynamic continues to be Jane Campion's 1999 film, *Holy Smoke*. At least in North America, the most egregious excesses of the anticult – including the criminal actions of Ted Patrick, the so-called father of deprogramming – have been recognized and condemned as the flagrant violations of civil liberties and religious freedom that they are. Nevertheless, the fact that the secular anticult still seeks to 'exit counsel' adherents indicates that its basic posture towards new religious involvement has changed very little.

Like its secular counterpart, the Christian countercult's definition of a cult and its theory of cultic behaviour exist in an inextricably tautological relationship, its explanation for the so-called cult explosion deriving all but inevitably from its fundamental principles. That is, because (a) the evangelical Christian worldview is *unique, exclusive,* and *insuperable,* this means that (b) an irresolvable *conflict of worldviews* exists between true Christians and all other religious believers, and, therefore, (c) à la Dave Hunt and others mentioned earlier in this Element, true Christians have an *inviolable mandate to convert* these benighted adherents of other faiths. Put differently, and unlike the secular anticult, which is responding to a particular moment in human religious history, countercult apologists see themselves as the latest regiment called up for active duty in a cosmological conflict that has been ongoing since the Fall.

In *The Culting of America*, for example, Ron Rhodes, who also worked with Martin at the CRI, believes that 'the cults in America are – to borrow a phrase from the military – a *clear and present danger*' (1994: 26; emphasis in the original). Like most of his countercult colleagues, because Rhodes insists that Christianity – specifically, conservative, evangelical Protestantism – 'rests on a foundation of absolute truth', a so-called cult or false religion is any group which does not conform to his particular faith vision (78; see Rhodes 1997: 301–8). This means that there is a mandate to convert, and that 'if Christians do not act, *the cults will. The war is on* – and you as a Christian will either be a soldier in the midst of the conflict or a casualty on the sidelines. Which will it be?' (Rhodes 1994: 219; emphasis in the original). Writing specifically in this instance about the New Age movement – though his characterization could be applied to any non-Christian tradition – evangelical philosopher Douglas Groothuis agrees, contending that 'despite whatever good intentions New Agers may have, it is Satan, the spiritual counterfeiter himself, who ultimately inspires all false religion' (1988: 38; see Groothuis 1996). Like Rhodes, Groothuis believes that Christians 'are involved in literal spiritual warfare', that their faith places them 'in combat conditions, with no demilitarized zones this side of heaven', and that his own co-religionists 'need to remember that the Christian witness to the New Ager' – for which, again, we might substitute any non-Christian believer – 'is a spiritual offensive into enemy territory' (1988: 39, 68).

The important point here is that for the Christian countercult, as well as for evangelical apologists more generally, the concept of spiritual warfare is not a metaphor. Rather, it is a deadly serious conflict involving a very real enemy in which eternal consequences are at stake. In this, the countercult cosmology is profoundly dualistic. Walter Martin, the Passantinos, Bob Larson, Constance Cumbey, Douglas Groothuis, and Ron Rhodes – indeed, many of those who have garrisoned Christian territory against a varied host of invaders – are not simply defenders of a particular view of the world; they perceive themselves in almost Manichaean terms, as warriors in a dualistic battle of light against darkness (Cowan 2003a: 46; for evangelical Christian fiction expounding precisely this point, see Peretti 1986, 1989).

'From the Christian perspective', wrote Ron Enroth more than a generation ago, 'the so-called new age cults represent the most recent manifestation of an age-old struggle – the battle between God and God's adversary, Satan' (1977: 202). This position has not changed. Nearly fifty years later, prospective members in EMNR must 'consent to and agree with the contents of the Lausanne Covenant', an affirmation of evangelical Christian doctrine produced in 1984 by the Lausanne Congress on World Evangelization. Article 12 states unequivocally: 'We believe that we are engaged in constant spiritual warfare with the principalities and powers of evil, who are seeking to overthrow the Church and frustrate its task of world evangelization' (Evangelical Ministries to Non-Christian Religions 2022). Dave Hunt bluntly declares in *A Woman Rides the Beast*, his own lengthy contribution to anti-Catholic apologetics, that 'the Bible says that there are two classes of people, those who are saved and those who are lost' (1994b: 347). While condemning Roman Catholicism for its doctrine of *extra ecclesiam nulla salus* (lit., 'outside the Church there is no salvation') countercult apologists such as Hunt rarely seem to notice that they are offering up their own version of precisely the same theological demarcation. Whether they are confronting Catholics or CaoDai, Asatruar or atheists, Muslims or modern pagans, 'the primary goal of evangelicals is to preach the gospel to the lost so they might be saved' (350) – because those are the stakes of the game.

Threat Perception: The Stakes of the Game

On the 2023 iteration of its website, the ICSA insists that it 'does not maintain a list of "bad" groups or "cults"'. Rather, and not unlike the Center for Apologetics Research, 'we nonjudgmentally list groups on which we have information' (n.d.). And, to be fair, the members of the ICSA may believe that this is the case, but like so much of the secular anticult's special pleading, it is difficult to know whether such statements are deliberately disingenuous, simply naïve, or intended to indemnify them against the kind of legal actions that bankrupted other anticult groups and personalities. More than that, since 'groups listed, described, or referred to in ICSA's archive may be mainstream or nonmainstream, controversial or noncontroversial, religious or nonreligious, cult or not a cult, harmful or benign', it is equally difficult to discern what purpose such a list is intended to serve – especially since the website banner reads, 'Cult Info since 1979' (International Cultic Studies Association n.d.). Beyond a standard disclaimer that 'views expressed on ICSA Websites are the author(s)', the vast majority of the groups actually listed have been specifically identified at one time or another as dangerous cults, are rhetorically linked with such groups, or are presented as potentially dangerous and thus bear closer scrutiny. Once again, though, the wide and ambiguous net cast by the secular anticult only increases the confusion.

Charlene Edge, for example, joined Victor Paul Wierwille's The Way International at age eighteen during her first year at college. She describes this as a time when 'Way recruiters swept me into their cult', as though she had no agency in the matter and only years later 'managed to escape before I was unmasked as a traitor' (2016). Indeed, Edge's article epitomizes the kind of anecdotal atrocity narrative that so closely reinforces the secular anticult's brain-washing/thought control thesis. 'Over time', she concludes, once she had left the group, 'I gained understanding about fundamentalism and the cult phenomenon I had experienced.' She credits 'mindfulness, a Buddhist practice, [for keeping] me grounded' as she has sought to recover from the experience (Edge 2016). Conversely, writing in the annual *International Journal of Coercion, Abuse, and Manipulation*, which is published by the ICSA and 'expands the mission of the *International Journal of Cultic Studies*', psychotherapist Sue Parker Hall cau-tioned the anticult community about the need for 'Being Mindful about Mindfulness: Exploring the Dark Side' (2020). While admitting that 'mindful-ness intervention works well as a standalone modality' – whatever that actually means – Hall is particularly concerned about 'the training, quality, and supervi-sion of mindfulness teachers', 'the consequences of its secularization, reduction, and commercialization', and 'the potential for abuse of mindfulness', especially when this is used in the 'recruitment of people into cults' – a term she defines only as 'high-demand groups' (Hall 2020: 17, 21). Thus, for one ICSA contributor mindfulness has contributed to her mental health and recovery, while for another it represents another avenue for potential abuse in cultic groups (28). In short, somebody might get hurt sometime by some group or other.

The common thread running through each of these, indeed through most if not all of the articles, blog posts, and sundry resources offered by the ICSA, is that the stakes of the game can be reduced to freedom of thought, conscience, and religious conviction, specifically the rights of people to be free from coercion, abuse, and manipulation in their pursuit of each – clearly an admirable goal with which, in principle at least, few could reasonably disagree. The problem, though, is that in practice, there is often little distinction between the real abuses encountered in the context of religious communities and the perception of abuse based on unpopular religious choices or a sense of 'buyer's remorse' once someone has left a suspect group. How do those in the secular ACM reliably distinguish one from the other? What is the algorithm by which they assess, per Canadian civil rights lawyer Alan Borovoy (1988), the inevitable collision of freedoms that their assessment of potential new religious threat represents? That is, when does freedom of religion get reduced to the freedom to make religious choices as long as either others agree with the choices you make or you don't regret them later on? Because of this, the secular anticult seems either to forget or to ignore that the litmus test of religious freedom is precisely the freedom for people to make religious choices with which others disagree – often vehemently and, occasionally, for very good reason – but to make them nonetheless.

The language of this conviction resonates throughout secular anticult literature, specifically in the antagonistic alarmism embedded in rhetoric contrasting captivity with freedom. This can be seen, for example, in Steven Hassan's 2000 book *Releasing the Bonds* (captivity) juxtaposed against its subtitle, *Empowering People to Think for Themselves* (freedom). Similarly, Madeline Tobias and Janja Lalich in 1994 opposed their book's title *Captive Hearts, Captive Minds* (captivity) against its subtitle *Freedom and Recovery from Cults and Other Abusive Relationships* (freedom). In a 2006 book, they show former NRM members how to *Take Back Your Life* (freedom) against captivity in the subtitle: *Recovering from Cults and Abusive Relationships*. Once again, and despite pallid disclaimers urging 'inquirers to avoid the temptation to oversimplify' and to 'make independent and informed judgments pertinent to their particular concerns' (International Cultic Studies Association n.d.), how is anyone coming to the ICSA for information expected to arrive at a different conclusion or a different assessment of the relative threat than that *there is* a threat?

Few in the anticult, especially those for whom anticult activism forms part or all of their professional identity, seem to realize the lengths to which they have become hostages to their own ideology. Indeed, in this, it is worth remembering the words of Friedrich Nietzsche, that 'convictions might be more dangerous enemies of truth than lies' (1895: 185; see 178–85). In fact, Nietzsche's thoughts on the nature of conviction fill the final, brief chapters of *The Anti-Christ*. 'Every conviction has its history', he writes, 'its preliminary forms, its tentative shapes, its blunders: it *becomes* a conviction after *not* being one for a long time, after *hardly* being one for an even longer time' (185). Put bluntly, he concludes, 'convictions are prisons', though those so imprisoned rarely if ever recognize this possibility (184).

While the Christian countercult is entrenched in similarly dogmatic fashion – religious belief is nothing if not humankind's most potent form of ideological conviction – if so-called cults or false religions abrogate the rights and freedoms of their adherents, it is not so much a cause for legal concern as it is concrete evidence of the satanic programme to take over the world and deny evangelical Christianity its rightful place as the one true faith. Rather than brainwashing, though, invasion, infiltration, and infection are the controlling metaphors. 'Of course', admits Ron Rhodes, 'there are no skull-and-crossbones POISON warning labels stamped on the cults – labels like those found on bottles containing deadly elements. Tragically, though, innumerable people in the United States are drinking down spiritual cyanide by the megadose' (1994: 26). Indeed, the phenomena of competitor religions, whether new or old, writes Ronald Enroth, 'are neither random nor accidental; they are profoundly patterned'. Lest anyone mistake his meaning, he concludes that, 'as simplistic as it may sound to some, they indicate a demonic conspiracy to subvert the true gospel of Jesus Christ through human agents whose eyes have been blinded by the evil one' (1977: 202).

In this regard, consider Buddhism and Hinduism, global religious traditions that, together, account for nearly 20 per cent of the world's population. 'If consumer laws of full disclosure were applied to "the sale" of religions', writes Bob Larson, 'Buddhism would probably have been left on the shelf' (1989: 72). Mahāyāna he dismisses as 'more of a cult religion utilizing incense, magic, and occult rituals', in which 'Buddha figures are objects of deified worship', while Theravada is reduced to a 'godless, virtually atheistic system' of belief (76). Vajrayana he derides as 'the most openly occult of all non-Christian world religions', denouncing the interest shown by its Western adherents and lamenting its 'growing foothold in North America' (79). 'Perhaps the demonic forces behind Tibetan Buddhism', he wonders, 'have deliberately prolonged [the Dalai Lama's] exile as a means of exporting this ancient, shamanistic faith' (79). Hinduism fares little better, with Larson arguing that its 'polytheistic and idolatrous practices are pagan forms of worship that constitute collusion with demonic forces' (70). Putting the case in even starker terms, Dave Hunt declares that 'Hindu-Buddhist philosophy was at the heart of Nazism' (1983: 143). With such other countercult writers as Constance Cumbey (1983) and Caryl

Matrisciana (1985), Hunt argues that Hinduism was directly responsible not only for the advent of Nazism, but also for the atrocities that followed in the Third Reich. Forging tenuous links between (a) the Aryan tribes that swept down into the subcontinent, bringing with them the beginnings of Hinduism, (b) the popularity in early twentieth-century Germany of certain aspects of Hinduism, particularly as these were transmitted through racialized Theosophical thought, and (c) a spurious connection between use of the *haken-kreuz*, the swastika, as the central Nazi symbol, Hunt unapologetically states that 'it was the Aryan god of Hinduism who willed Hitler upon the world' (152).

While few countercult writers take as bleak a view of Hinduism as Cumbey, Matrisciana, and Hunt, they all consider it no less a clear and present danger. Beginning with 'the avalanche of Hindu gurus and swamis who invaded the United States in the 1960s and 1970s' (Marrs 1990: 216), especially through Transcendental Meditation and the International Society for Krishna Consciousness, the floodgates were opened. Some see Hinduism's most significant infiltration, to use one of Ron Rhodes' favourite words (1994: 21), through yoga. Indeed, 'yoga *is* Hinduism', writes Jill Rische, Walter Martin's eldest daughter, who has continued his work. 'It cannot be separated from it. Those who argue that it is simply good exercise do not understand the history of it' (Martin, Rische, and Van Gorden 2008: 317). Published nearly two decades after Martin's death, written with another CRI alum, Kurt van Gorden, *Kingdom of the Occult* both trades on Walter Martin's name recognition in the countercult community and continues his legacy as a significant movement intellectual. Of particular concern for Rische is that 'today, the practice of Yoga has invaded the Church to the point where some pastors actually hold yoga classes in their sanctuaries' (317). Interpreted as yet one more aspect of the 'occult revolution', another front in the ongoing spiritual war, yoga was 'created specifically for the worship of Hindu gods' (318). As far as Rische and van Gorden are concerned, it is neither 'a substitute for aerobics' nor 'intended to be used for physical activity alone; it was created to worship deities the Bible calls *demons*' (319; emphasis in the original).

'I joined a yoga class for fitness and relaxation,' writes one contributor to Dave Hunt's *Berean Call* newsletter. 'Drop the class immediately!' Hunt replies. 'Yoga is the very heart of Hinduism.' 'During the class, mantras are used,' the letter continues. 'Can I just substitute Christian words such as "Jesus"?' 'Substitute Jesus as your "Christian mantra"?' Hunt thunders. 'No!' Seeming not to notice the internal inconsistency in his answer, he continues, 'Yoga teachers all declare that the repetition of a mantra is a call to that god (i.e., the demon it represents) to come and possess the meditator. I have interviewed people who became demon possessed through yoga' (Hunt 1998b: 4).

Since the stakes could hardly be higher, what then to do?

Resolution: Coercing Exit or Compelling Conversion

If there is one thing upon which both the secular anticult and the Christian countercult can agree, it is that men, women, and children who are involved in problematic or dangerous religious groups are in need of rescue. In the same way that they differ on what constitutes problematic or renders this group or that dangerous, however, the means by which the anticult and the countercult approach the issue of resolution is, at least in North America, very different. Put simply, for the former, the objective is exit, for the latter conversion.

It is important to note, however, that in many other countries, the issue is not nearly so clear-cut. Although deprogramming was technically outlawed in Japan in 2015, for example, persistent concerns about such groups as the Family Federation for World Peace and Unification (formerly known as the Unification Church) has prompted calls for it to be legalized and more widely used. In Brazil, fundamentalist Christians routinely and often violently target Afro-Brazilian religions such as Candomblé and Umbanda, calling their adherents 'Satanists' (see Introvigne 2022a, 2022c). In South Korea, kidnapping and forcible deprogramming continues to occur, targeting members of the Shincheonji Church (the Temple of the Tabernacle of the Testimony), an unorthodox Christian NRM founded in the mid-1980s. In this case, however, rather than a secular anticult, 'the phenomenon of coercive change of religion in South Korea is exclusively carried out by fundamentalist Protestant Churches', for the most part conservative Presbyterians associated with the Christian Cult Counselling Association of Korea (Fautré 2020: 37). Although Shincheonji has been the major target of these activities, we should note that it is not the only one (see also Di Marzio 2020; Introvigne 2021; Richardson 2011).

For the secular ACM in North America, however, once the forcible deprogramming of the 1970s was declared illegal and, in many cases, successfully prosecuted, the practice gave way to less invasive and more sophisticated (but arguably no less offensive) forms of exit counselling. Today, the secular anticult frames its activities in terms of information exchange and referral, therapeutic exit intervention, and family support. However it is characterized, though, counselling, coercing, or cajoling *exit* remains the primary goal when dealing with new religion adherents whose human rights or civil liberties the secular anticult considers to have been compromised, then facilitating some form of reintegration into family and society. Whether someone leaves the Church of Scientology and becomes a Blue Army Catholic, for example, is of little concern. Whether former believers recognize that, following their time with the Moonies or Hare Krishna or The Family International, they decide to enter the ranks of the 'nones', and claim to be either 'spiritual but not religious' or even confirmed atheists, is of no moment as far as the secular anticult is concerned. They are out of the problematic group, and that is all that matters.

For the Christian countercult, when it comes to interaction with a member of any religion other than evangelical Protestantism, the goal of any encounter is to convince the believer that he/she is part of a cult, false religion, or other suspect spiritual tradition, and then encourage him/her to convert. That is, *exit* provides only part of the solution. True salvation is not achieved until the person has converted to whatever form of Christianity grounds the countercult apologetics. Whereas secular anticult tactics have included arguments against the beliefs and practices of specific groups, Christian countercult motivation proceeds along two mutually supportive paths: *apologetics as evangelism* and *apologetics as reality-maintenance* (see Section 4).

In terms of apologetics as evangelism, whether deliberate or accidental, the goal of any conversation, debate, or encounter with people of different religions is 'to provide well-reasoned evidences to the non-believer as to why he ought to choose Christianity rather than any other religion. Apologetics can be used to show the unbeliever that all the other options in the smorgasbord of world religions *are not really options at all*, because they are false' (Rhodes 1994: 230; emphasis in the original). Consider carefully Rhodes' use of language: *non-believer* and *unbeliever*. Even recognizing that Rhodes means 'non-Christian', how likely is it that followers of any religious tradition would respond positively to such a characterization, indeed, would not see it as simply insulting? Douglas Groothuis takes it further, arguing for a species of 'negative apologetics' which explicitly 'presents *reasons against* non-Christian perspectives' (Groothuis 1988: 67; emphasis in the original). That is, apologists are urged to confront so-called non-believers, telling them bluntly, 'Your perspective doesn't make sense; and it doesn't fit the facts. Therefore you shouldn't believe it' (67).

A number of countercult apologists recognize the problem with this kind of aggressive evangelization, however much they may agree with Rhodes and Groothuis' theological position. Anxiety about confronting those who believe differently, embarrassment over the implicit arrogance of the countercult position, even fear of the not-unreasonable backlash one might encounter when approaching, say, a family of Latter-day Saints with the good news that everything their faith has taught them is wrong and yours is right – all these have led to significant concerns about the value of countercult evangelism.

'Apologetics isn't argumentative,' insists Alan Shlemon, a speaker and writer with the apologetics organization Stand to Reason, the motto for which is 'Clear Thinking Christianity' – 'at least, it shouldn't be' (2020). Rather, Christian believers should 'distinguish *apologetics* and the *manner in which it is practiced*'

(2020). In an accompanying 'apologetics tip for the day', Shlemon adds, 'We can make a case for our moral or religious convictions by stating our view and providing evidence for it. And we don't have to be aggressive, harsh, or mean about it. And that way, we come across as a winsome and gracious ambassador for Christ' (Shlemon 2019). All of which is almost certainly true, but the message conveyed is still rather brutally clear. According to Stand to Reason's statement of faith: 'The whole human race fell in the Fall of the first Adam' and 'are justified on the simple and single ground of the shed blood of Christ and upon the simple and single condition of faith in Him' (Art. 9, 10). 'All those who persistently reject Jesus Christ' will be 'punished for their moral crimes and rebellion against God' (Art. 11). However winsomely and graciously the message is presented, the message itself is still the same: 'Throughout eternity they' – all those who do not accept this particular version of the Christian gospel – 'will exist in a state of conscious isolation from God, in endless torment and anguish' (Art. 11). Once again, we have the countercult version of *extra ecclesiam nulla salus*: Accept our religious vision or risk eternal, conscious punishment.

In the end, whether apologetics is presented in the openly fire-and-brimstone manner of Dave Hunt or with the disarming folksiness of Alan Shlemon doesn't really matter. In Stand to Reason's 'Statement of Values', while 'honesty and integrity' are important, while 'accuracy, clarity, and even-handedness' are embraced as cardinal virtues, 'faithfulness over results' is paramount. 'Our first call is to be faithful to Christ, who alone can bring the increase. Results are a secondary, not primary, measure of our efforts' (Stand to Reason 2022).

What, then, *is* primary? Leaving aside comparisons between the secular anticult and the Christian countercult, this brings us to the principal reason for the latter's entrenched interest in and resistance towards new, alternative, or competing religious faiths: reality-maintenance and the primacy of the evangelical Protestant worldview.

4 Reality-Maintenance and the Christian Countercult Movement

Bill McKeever and his Mormonism Research Ministry may organize witnessing events at the opening of new LDS stake centres, local churches may host WF staffers for a four-day 'Area-Wide Cult Impact Conference', and individual believers may engage, however winsomely, with Jehovah's Witnesses or Mormons when they knock on the door, but the reality is that most of those who consume countercult literature will not. And yet supply and demand for this kind of material continue unabated among evangelical Christians. There must, therefore, be another reason for its popularity. To explain this, we need to recall Boa and Bowman's three principles of apologetics: 'a *defense* of Christianity as a system, a *vindication* of the Christian worldview against its assailants, and a *refutation* of opposing systems and theories' (Boa and Bowman 2001: 20).

Despite oft-repeated claims of religious believers to the contrary, no reality is more socially constructed than the religious, no worldview more open to the challenge of faith-based pluralism, and, consequently, none more in need of ongoing maintenance, reinforcement, and validation. Tens of millions of evangelical Christians see themselves beset on all sides by conflicting interpretations of their own faith, by other religions from around the world, by a welter of competing life philosophies, as well as by emergent, unconventional, and often intimidating new spiritual paths. As Berger and Luckmann point out, neatly capturing the problem, for any socially constructed reality even 'the appearance of an alternative symbolic universe poses a threat because its very existence demonstrates empirically that one's own universe is less than inevitable' (1966: 126).

For example, what are Bible-believing Christians, those who accept that 'the Scriptures of the Old and New Testament are without error or misstatement in their moral and spiritual teachings and record of historical facts' ('Statement of Faith' 2022), to do when Exodus 22:18 clearly commands that 'Thou shalt not suffer a witch to live,' yet they live in a culture that not only suffers self-proclaimed witches to live, but also allows them to open bookshops, hold public rituals, and claim their place as legitimate partners at society's religious round-table (see Cowan and Bromley 2015: 161–80)? What are they to do when the local Scientology org bolts its placard to the municipal signboard and the town council won't do anything about it? What are they to do when their child returns from school with a new best friend, perhaps a young Hindu girl or little Mormon boy? In the face of these and a multitude of other perceived threats, the CCM provides an important prop for the ongoing appearance of evangelical Christian inevitability. It simply tells believers that they are right – and why.

Defense: Countercult Apologetics As Reality-Maintenance

If the first principle of apologetics is to establish that religious belief is more rational than non-belief, countercult apologetics defends the Christian cosmology against competing versions of reality. All other religious (and non-religious) systems and explanations are placed in the cosmological balance and ultimately found wanting. Specifically, though, 'since people join cults because of needs in their lives', writes Alan Gomes, the general editor of Zondervan's Guide to Cults and Religious Movements series, 'the best way to keep them out of the cults is to meet those needs *legitimately*, through Christ' (1998a: 96; emphasis added). By definition, then, all other spiritual pathways are *illegitimate* and only need to be so demonstrated. This exposes the fundamental difference between apologetics-as-evangelism and apologetics-as-reality-maintenance.

In an evangelical encounter, apologists are faced not only with the question of competing interpretations of reality, but also the fact that other religious believers simply may not accept the grounds on which the apologists seek to make their case. That is, while they may recognize that the Bible is important to Christians, they may not accept it as having any claim on their religious imagination at all. In the domain of apologetics-as-reality-maintenance, however, this problem is obviated, since common acceptance of the Bible as the 'inspired, infallible, inerrant, and literal Word of God' (Marrs 1990: 56) is the 'general axiom' (Mannheim 1952: 146) from which all other aspects of countercult cosmology derive. It is an understood epistemic circularity that led the philosopher Ken Wilber to imagine a conversation that proceeds, '"What is the most sacred and authoritative book ever written in the world?" "The Bible." "How do you know?" "It says so in the Bible." This may sound odd', Wilber concludes puckishly, 'but that is not my fault' (1993: 21). While countercult apologists may go to great lengths to establish the authority of the Bible in the context of establishing an evangelistic foothold, in terms of reality-maintenance, that authority is taken for granted.

In *Truth and Error*, for example, a summary volume in the Zondervan series, Gomes reprises some of the basic information found in each of the individual contributions, presenting them in terms of 'Comparative Charts of Cults and Christianity'. Down one column he lists various bits and pieces of a group's religious history, belief, doctrine, and sources of inspiration, then places what he considers a countermanding verse from the Bible in the opposing column. That '[neo-]Pagans recognize the divinity of nature and of all living things', for example, is simply contrasted with Deuteronomy 4:35: 'You were shown these things that you might know that the LORD is God; besides him there is no other' (Gomes 1998a: 70; cf. Jones and Matthews 1990). While 'divination in all its forms has always been an important part of the witch's craft', Revelation 21:8 warns solemnly that, among others, for 'those who practice magic arts . . . their place will be in the fiery lake of burning sulphur. This is the second death' (Gomes 1998a: 74; cf. Valiente 1973). Gomes juxtaposes Margot Adler's creative misreading of Luke 17:21 (not to mention Saying 3 of the Gospel of Thomas) – 'The kingdom of God is within you' – with the words of Acts 4:12: 'Salvation is found in no one else, for there is no other name under heaven given to men by which we must be saved' (Gomes 1998a: 73; cf. Adler 1986). In all instances, as far as Gomes' presumed reader is concerned, case closed.

For the most part, and unlike many of his countercult colleagues, Gomes does quote directly from reputable sources for these other traditions, but they are offered as though existing sui generis, with neither historical nor literary context, nor with any concern for theological development, institutional difference, or regional variation. He freely mixes fragments chosen from journalistic accounts (e.g., Adler) with cherry-picked passages from different scriptural traditions (e.g., the *Bhagavad Gita* or the *Analects* of Confucius) with no regard whatsoever for their differences. And, like so many countercult apologists, he lumps together such richly diverse religious and philosophical traditions as Buddhism, Confucianism, Taoism, and 'other far eastern religions' as though they can be considered all of a piece. The important point, however, is that in the context of countercult apologetics-as-reality-maintenance, they *can be* consolidated in precisely this manner – because any differences between them simply do not matter.

In similar fashion, Gomes deploys Bible verses with no regard for historical background, narrative arrangement, literary form, or theological context – again, because none of these things actually matter. It is enough to set one against the other because the conclusion is predetermined. Like aggrieved and confused parents who reach out to the ICSA already convinced that this or that religious group is evil, the countercult is predisposed to reject anything that does not conform to very specific biblical exegeses and extrapolations. All a countercult apologist such as Gomes needs to do is demonstrate that religious texts or practices differ from the Bible – however superficial or specious the comparison – and this confirms for the believer the illegitimacy of whatever group is under consideration. If it were otherwise, his evangelical readers would be placed in the uncomfortable and untenable position of denying the authority of Scripture, something that would gravely destabilize the foundation of their beliefs.

Lest readers of this Element think that this form of argumentation exists only on the fringes of evangelicalism, consider Gomes' credentials. Although Dave Hunt may have been a popular if slightly outré member of the CCM and Walter Martin a driving force but one who remained outside the educational mainstream of the evangelical church, Alan Gomes is currently professor of systematic and historical theology at Talbot School of Theology at Biola University, one of the most influential private Christian universities in North America. While Hunt's education (BA in mathematics and a prior career as a CPA) did little to prepare him for countercult apologetics and Martin's credentials have been suspect for decades, Gomes' academic preparation is solidly evangelical and beyond reproach. But his message is no different and is presented with no more attention to nuance than that of either Hunt or Martin.

Arguably the most common form of confirmation bias, reality-maintenance is about supporting the belief that the world-as-you-believe-it-to-be corresponds in fact to the world-as-it-is. This support comes through pointing out the flaws in other worldviews, with the implicit (if flawed) understanding that doing so demonstrates the correctness of one's own interpretation. What happens, though, when evangelical believers are confronted by those with whom they ostensibly share a worldview, who to all appearances believe the same things?

Vindication: Countercult Apologetics As Worldview Reinforcement

If countercult *reality-maintenance* is about confirming a Christian cosmological vision against competing interpretations of reality, *worldview reinforcement* narrows the apologetic focus, buttressing belief in a particular version of Christianity, in this case, evangelical Protestantism. While reality-maintenance confronts religious belief that does not accept the Bible, world-view reinforcement challenges those whose views of the Bible are deemed incorrect. This may seem a distinction without much of a difference, but consider this a reaction to divergent theologies rather than opposition to differing cosmologies. If, as Gomes asserts, countercult apologetics entails convincing people to approach the Divine 'legitimately, through Christ', worldview reinforcement asks the question: 'Okay, but *whose* Christ?'

Although countercult apologists lay claim to legitimacy through a variety of terms – support for the cardinal doctrines of the historic Christian faith, adherence to biblical or traditional Christianity – their opposition to internal religious competitors often hinges on the word 'orthodox'. While these other terms may be open to varying interpretations, 'orthodox' is a concrete signifier of authentic Christian identity. 'Historic', for instance, could easily be contrasted with 'modern' or 'contemporary', 'traditional' with 'nontraditional' or 'unconventional'. On the other hand, 'orthodoxy' (i.e., 'correct belief') functions only as a correlative of 'heterodoxy' (i.e., 'different belief'), or as it is colloquially understood across the apologetic spectrum, *incorrect* belief or *heresy*. 'Objective truth is the plumb line', writes Sue Cyre, 'which divides truth and falsehood, creating a boundary' (1995: 1). 'To affirm truth', the former executive director of Presbyterians for Faith, Family and Ministry, and editor of its bimonthly journal, *Theology Matters*, continues, 'we must identify what is false. If we attempt to reaffirm orthodoxy without rediscovering heresy we deny the boundaries and we embrace the syncretism of pagan religions' (2).

Indeed, by deploying the language of correct belief, Christian countercult apologists stake a normative claim to their own particular interpretation of the gospel message. That is, by ignoring the long and complicated history of the concept, including those denominations that explicitly claim it as part of their identity and heritage, the countercult equates orthodox with conservative, evangelical Protestant. By defining their position as orthodox, they declare that theirs is the only acceptable answer to the central questions of Christian identity and ultimate salvation, and theirs the only legitimate description of the mysterious relationship between the human and the divine. The importance of this conceptual and terminological detail ought not be underestimated. While signifiers such as traditional and historic do not necessarily imply an inauthentic religious Other, 'orthodox' demands it. As the benchmark of doctrinal, ethical, and soteriological veracity, it exists only in opposition to heresy and heterodoxy. In fact, orthodoxy demands heresy as the means by which its own boundaries are delineated, and one's own identity as a legitimate Christian claimed. In the language of spiritual warfare, if other religions constitute the *enemy*, deviant interpretations of the same faith identify the *traitors* in the midst of God's house. And, as any soldier will tell you, traitors are infinitely more dangerous than enemies.

'*Whose* Christ?' you ask. '*Our* Christ,' the countercult replies.

The countercult is alarmed at what it considers to be the infiltration of the 'true' Christian church by a variety of heresies: 'creeping syncretism' (in the form of ecumenical dialogue), 'scientific materialism' (which will, apparently, lead to first contact with extraterrestrial intelligence), a 'basic occult belief that mind creates its own reality', and, worst of all, an outright apostasy that clearly marks the beginning of the end times (Hunt and McMahon 1985: 93, 186). Dave Hunt and former Roman Catholic Tom McMahon called out their fellow religionists on these very issues in the controversial though bestselling *Seduction of Christianity* (1985). Two years later, *Beyond Seduction: A Return to Biblical Christianity* reinforced their point and, in no uncertain terms, answered their numerous critics (1987; for evangelical responses, see, e.g., DeMar and Leithart 1988; Paulk 1987; Reid et al. 1986). Although Hunt and McMahon were concerned about any religious group that challenged the dominance of their very particular version of evangelical Christianity, in language that echoes the anti-Catholic nativism of the nineteenth century, they reserved some of their most heated rhetoric for the Church of Rome.

In 'A Cult Is a Cult', for example, Hunt expressed his anger that most of his fellow apologists – notably Walter Martin – did not bundle Roman Catholicism together with Jehovah's Witnesses, Latter-day Saints, and Christian Scientists. That is,

> [T]he most seductive, dangerous, and largest cult (many times larger than all the rest combined) is not included in the list! Most cult experts refuse to identify this horrendous cult as such! Instead, they accept is as 'Christian'. Worst of all, this cult (which preaches a *false* gospel that is sending hundreds of millions into a Christless eternity) is now embraced as a partner in 'evangelizing the world' by many groups which preach the biblical gospel! ... No cult demands surrender of mind and conscience more fully or arrogantly than Roman Catholicism. (Hunt 1991: 1)

Three years later, in an article in his *Berean Call* newsletter, Hunt implored readers 'to weep for and seek to win for the gospel not only those trapped in the well-known cults, but the [then] 980 million Roman Catholics held in the grip of a false gospel that sends them to hell' (Hunt 1994a: 2).

Nearly a generation later, this position has not changed. Indeed, in 2018, five years after Hunt's death, McMahon published 'Biblically Thinking about Catholicism: Tradition vs. Scripture', a thirty-five-page booklet in his Berean Bites series, much of which simply reprints many of the anti-Catholic passages from Hunt's earlier work. The back cover banner points to what many in the CCM consider a hallmark of this particularly dangerous cult: 'The "Christ" of Roman Catholicism is just as false as its "Mary"' (McMahon 2018). While evangelical apologists take issue with many aspects of Roman Catholicism, arguably what most offends their theological sensibilities is the exaltation and veneration of the Virgin Mary.

As far as Hunt and McMahon are concerned, Mary has quite simply replaced Jesus as both the focus of worship and the locus of salvation for Roman Catholics. They contend that she has become even more important than God because 'when Mary commands even God obeys' (Hunt 1994b: 446). In *Reasoning from the Scriptures with Catholics*, Ron Rhodes spends more time refuting the doctrine of Mary than on any other aspect of Roman Catholic theology, and on most others combined. In *Mary: Another Redeemer?*, James White warns Protestants and Catholics alike about the Church of Rome's 'controversial movement to name Mary as co-redeemer with Christ' (1998). Similarly, in *The Fatal Flaw*, tellingly subtitled *Do the Teachings of Roman Catholicism Deny the Gospel?* White proclaims unapologetically, 'the Roman Catholic Church's teaching on the work of Jesus Christ (specifically His atonement) is anti-Biblical and false; hence the Roman Catholic Church is not in possession of the Gospel of Jesus Christ, and cannot, therefore, be considered a Christian church' (White 1990: 19; see Cowan 2003a: 171–89). In an attempt to 'love the sinner, but hate the sin', White cautions his 'Christian reader' that 'the evil of Roman Catholicism lies in the system, not, by and large, the individuals who are part of it. Only a small percentage of Roman Catholics are actively involved in promulgating falsehood. The vast majority are simply deceived' (White 1990: 190).

Once again, though, it does not matter in the least if any of these anti-Catholic claims are true in fact; they contribute to the statement of faith upon which tens of millions of evangelical Christians have built their theological house. But if a religious organization that counts as members one out of every six persons on the planet and that proclaims itself, in the words of the Catechism, 'the place "where the Spirit flourishes"', is in reality 'not in possession of the Gospel' and all but a small constituency 'simply deceived', then what is it? For many countercult apologists the Roman Catholic Church is a prophetic affirmation, a worldwide religious institution that validates some of their most ardent hopes for the end of the world.

Affirmation: Countercult Apologetics As Prophetic Validation

The fifth fundamental – belief in the literal and visible second coming of Christ – describes the common sentiment among evangelical Protestants that a believer's earthly life is merely a waypoint on their journey towards an eternity with God. For hundreds of millions of these believers, that journey is almost over. That is, we are living in the end times and the presence of everything from yoga practice in the local United Church of Canada to the millions of Catholics who each year make their pilgrimage to Fatima, Lourdes, and Medjugorje constitute proof that the Rapture and the Tribulation to follow are just around the corner.

In both *Global Peace and the Rise of Antichrist* (1990) and *A Woman Rides the Beast* (1994b), Dave Hunt presents the most negative interpretation possible of Roman Catholic history in support of his belief that the Roman Catholic Church will herald the ascension of the Antichrist and constitute the seat of power for a revived Roman Empire, a staple of fundamentalist end times conspiracism. This view is shared by thousands of Hunt's co-religionists, if letters to the editor in *The Berean Call* are any indication. This is nothing new or limited to countercult apologists such as Hunt and McMahon. In the wake of the Leipzig Debate of 1519, for example, the papal bull *Exsurge domine* threatened Martin Luther with excommunication and forbade 'every one of the faithful of either sex' under similar penalty of excommunication 'to read, assert, preach, praise, print, publish, or defend' more than forty of Luther's ninety-five theses. This led Luther to change his views on the Antichrist, who was no longer a prophetic figure consigned to the distant future, but one located in the papal apartments of the Vatican. Five hundred years later, the conservative Wisconsin Evangelical Lutheran Synod – the church of which American politician and 2012 presidential candidate Michele Bachmann was a long-time member – asserted unequivocally in its Doctrinal Statement on the Antichrist that 'the Papacy is the Antichrist' (2022; see Green 2011).

Whereas countercult apologists such as Ron Rhodes and James White object to the veneration of Mary on theological grounds, Hunt and McMahon (the latter of whom continues to propagate these views long after Hunt's death) see in her a principal point of eschatological fulfillment. She is both the 'woman who rides the beast' and the 'whore of Babylon'. This interpretation is only reinforced by the thread of misogyny woven throughout much of Hunt's work. 'Today's women are asserting themselves as never before in history,' he writes, something that only confirms for him the problem (1994b: 456). As far as he is concerned, the evidence of the approaching end is overwhelming: 'women instigate more domestic violence' than men; 'women are taking over what were once men's jobs'; 'there is a growing acceptance of women at the highest levels of leadership in business, government, and religion' (456). From all this he concludes that 'only God could have given [the apostle] John, 1900 years ago, a vision that so fits our day – a *woman* in control' (456). Indeed, 'from the current trends, it seems inevitable that a *woman* must ride the beast' (456; emphases in the original). That the 'last-days' Babylon is described as a *woman* again identifies her as the Roman Catholic Church, for whom a *woman* – the 'Virgin Mary' – is the dominant deity. Though many Catholics would deny it, she has taken the place of God and Christ. (Hunt 1990: 120; emphases in the original)

Hunt goes on to condemn Marian apparitions at such sites as Fatima, Lourdes, and Medjugorje as 'blasphemy of the worst kind [for which] the satanic delusion is undeniable' (1994b: 463). His biblicist logic epitomizes the manner in which scripture so often informs countercult apologetics. 'A "child Jesus" sometimes appears (at Fatima, etc.) with Mary. Jesus was a mature man when he died for our sins, and is resurrected and glorified at the Father's right hand . . . Obviously, then, the appearance of any "child Jesus" is demonic' (Hunt 1999: 4).

Essentially repeating the same argument, McMahon laments that 'although mankind is being drawn into every kind of spiritual deception in the last days before the return of Jesus, it is especially sad that the real mother of Jesus, the remarkable "handmaid of the Lord", is so terribly misrepresented, thereby drawing millions away from her Son' (2000: 6). One can only imagine how many millions of Roman Catholics would agree – though for obviously different reasons.

As odd as many of these arguments may sound to those who do not share them, unlike the secular anticult position, which is riddled with its own logical inconsistencies, the theological genius of Christian countercult apologetics is that it is entirely non-falsifiable. That is, apologetics-as-evangelism and apologetics-as-reality-maintenance are mutually reinforcing, no matter the outcome of either. If an evangelistic encounter is successful and a Catholic converts to evangelical Protestantism or a yoga practitioner leaves his/her mat behind, this is celebrated as faithful obedience to the Great Commission and evidence for the work of the Holy Spirit in that person's life. If it is not successful, then that simply reinforces the reality that evangelical Christians are living in the end times, further evidence for the truth of Jesus' words that 'many false prophets will arise and lead many astray' (Matthew 24:11).

How much higher could the stakes be?

5 The Future of the Christian Countercult

In the early 1990s, Jason Scott, an eighteen-year-old member of the United Pentecostal Church International, was kidnapped and forcibly detained by Rick Ross, a deprogrammer associated with the secular anticult organization Cult Awareness Network (CAN). After nearly a week of confinement and deprogramming, Scott escaped, but no charges were filed against Ross or his associates at the time. Arrested two years later for the crimes, Ross was acquitted of unlawful imprisonment in a criminal trial, but a civil suit resulted in nearly $5 million in damages against him, his accomplices, and CAN. In 1996, both Ross and CAN declared bankruptcy and CAN's assets, logo, and name were all purchased by the Church of Scientology. As NRM scholar J. Gordon Melton notes, 'the demise of CAN brought to an end (at least in North America) the cult wars' (2006: 139).

However, elsewhere in the world conflicts between anticult activists and new religion adherents continue. In Spain, for example, lawyer and legal scholar Carlos Bardávio Antón seeks to revive the brainwashing hypothesis in terms of legal statutes and to criminalize what he characterizes as coercive persuasion. He proposes prison sentences, presumably for group leaders, lasting from eight to fourteen years, and prohibiting employment for about the same length of time. He suggests in 'cases of serious imprudence', though this goes undefined, that the prison term should be only one to four years and a £100,000 fine (Antón 2020: 70). Antón's proposal suffers from all the problems inherent in the anticult approach, particularly how to reliably and impartially adjudicate when coercive persuasion has occurred. Aspects of the secular anticult may very well diminish, especially in liberal secular democracies where religious freedom is valued and, despite its pop cultural resonance, the influence of the brainwashing hypothesis continues to wane. But there is no indication that the Christian countercult will similarly decline. This is the final difference between the two movements.

Because the CCM is based on fundamentally different philosophical, epistemological, and, indeed, soteriological principles and axioms than its secular counterpart, the theological exclusivity of its evangelical Christianity virtually guarantees its survival. The spiritual war is ongoing, and countercult apologists will always be on the ramparts, alert for new threats and watching for fresh targets. This is not to say that it has not had its share of controversies. 'An entire book could be devoted to the social histories and internecine conflicts of various organizations in the Christian countercult' (Cowan 2003a: 197). The innate urge to locate and expose theological deviance cannot help but spill over into a variety of internal snipe hunts over conflicts real and imagined.

Questions have often been raised, for example, about the qualifications and credentials of countercult apologists ranging from Dave Hunt and Tom McMahon (Wise 1986) to Walter Martin (Brown and Brown 1981–95) and James White (Novak n.d.; see Cowan 2003a: 199–205). Others, especially in the open-source countercult environment of the Internet, have simply declared themselves experts, whether they possess any expertise or not. Following Walter Martin's death, internal struggles at CRI and disputes over direction and leadership led to a number of conflicts, most centred around the legitimacy of Martin's successor, Hank Hanegraff. This led, among other things, to conflicts with Martin's family, as well as lawsuits filed by more than thirty former CRI employees – who organized themselves into the Group for CRI Accountability – against Hanegraff himself for such alleged breaches as wrongful termination, abuse of authority, and financial mismanagement. He was also accused of plagiarism, misrepresentation both of his ordination credentials and of his consistent claim to being Martin's hand-picked successor (see Cowan 2003a: 195–7). Since that time, however, Hanegraff's position at the organization has only solidified to the point where his is now the name most prominently associated with the organization and CRI itself has become 'little more than a clearinghouse for "Hank Hanegraff, Inc."' (Cowan 2003a: 195).

Despite this, and unlike the secular anticult, which is restricted in many countries by legal statute and hampered by its lack of proactive ideological foundation, the Christian countercult will only continue to grow in the context of societies that are both increasingly secular and increasingly multireligious – precisely because both of these put their own theological beliefs at risk. We return to the question of what's at stake. The concept of religious freedom, which many countercult activists see as the constitutional mandate for their faith-based crusade, ensures that their activism will continue, and with it an inevitable conflict of freedoms.

A Conflict of Freedoms

'Evangelism can't be disrespectful by virtue of the fact that the Bible commands it,' blogged Alan Shlemon the day I was drafting this section. While Shlemon recognizes that other religious believers might feel insulted – and he understands why – the non-falsifiable countercult logic assures his readers of their righteousness. 'If Christians are only considering God's perspective', he continues, 'then they can rest assured that God is not displeased with their efforts' (Shlemon 2022). Others take what could be considered a more controversial approach.

Tennessee-based televangelists John Ankerberg and John Weldon, for example, insist that 'responsible religious freedom' demands 'a national discussion over how we protect legitimate religious freedoms and simultaneously protect ourselves from "freedom of religion"' (1999: xxviii). What they mean – and this is a view millions of their co-religionists share – is that the First Amendment ought to guarantee just enough freedom for people to choose to be Christian. Within the context of the CCM, the logic here is unassailable: 'since countercult apologists regard theirs as the only authentic religious path, and regard all others as false religions, true religious freedom can logically be found only in Christianity' (Cowan 2003a: 101). If people choose otherwise, warn Ankerberg and Weldon, 'God may have ordained a built-in penalty that could not be avoided should we forsake our foundations and responsibilities' (1999: xxix).

While the theological foundations of the CCM are located at least implicitly in *The Fundamentals*, its missional responsibilities derive from the Great Commission (Matthew 28:16–20). Many apologists defend not only their responsibility to evangelize others – whether those others want it or not – but their right to do so. If this right is contested, if other religious groups protest the often gross mischaracterizations of their own faith by the CCM or the presence of countercult evangelists at their events, Christian apologists not infrequently point to this resistance as an infringement of *their* First Amendment freedoms. Reinterpreting the concept of tolerance, some apologists argue that it is, in fact, *intolerant* to suggest that they cannot criticize other religions on the basis of their own religious beliefs. Although WF, for example, claims to endorse 'the rights of everyone to hold and practice divergent beliefs', it is nevertheless 'compelled to exercise its freedoms', both 'to expose questionable doctrines' and 'to offer spiritual alternatives in the form of traditional Christian faith' ('Mission Statement' n.d.; see also Roberts 2000).

More than three decades have passed since I walked into that small Christian bookstore on Vancouver Island and picked up *The Godmakers*, yet a review of current countercult materials demonstrates that very little has changed in the interim. And, given what is at stake for those evangelical believers who haunt this particular subculture, we should not imagine that it would. Given the increase in secularism (though not to anywhere near the degree predicted by early theorists of secularization; see Hadden 1987) and the decrease in religious interest and attendance (whether this equates to secularism or simply indicates a rise in those who consider themselves 'spiritual but not religious'), the perception of threat to the evangelical Christian worldview has not changed. Indeed, if countercult apologists are to be believed, it has only increased. Although some seem to be trying to soften their approach, the basic principles underpinning the CCM remain: an exclusive religious vision, predicated on a literalist understanding and interpretation of the Bible, animated by a specific epistemology and teleology and an unshakeable confidence in the righteousness of its cause and the correctness of its faith.

References

'About CFAR'. 2022. *Centers for Apologetics Research*; https://thecenters.org/about.aspx, accessed 2 December 2022.

'About Us'. 2022. *Resurse Crestina Românesti*; www.rcrwebsite.com/desprenoi.htm, accessed 3 December 2022.

Adler, M. 1986. *Drawing Down the Moon: Witches, Druids, Goddess-Worshippers and Other Pagans in America Today*. Rev. ed. Boston, MA: Beacon Press.

'Africa Centre for Apologetics Research'. *Centers for Apologetics Research*; https://thecenters.org/acfar.aspx, accessed 3 December 2022.

Almendros, C., R. Dubrow-Marshall, and S. K. D. Eichel et al. 2013. 'Dialogue and Cultic Studies: Why Dialogue Benefits the Cultic Studies Field. A Message from the Directors of ICSA Today'. *ICSA Today* 4, no. 3: 2–7; www.icsahome.com/articles/dialogue-and-cultic-studies-icsa-board-it-4-3, accessed 5 November 2022.

Ankarloo, B. and S. Clark, eds. 1999. *Witchcraft and Magic in Europe: The Twentieth Century*. Philadelphia: University of Pennsylvania Press.

Ankerberg, J. and J. Weldon. 1991. *Cult Watch*. Eugene, OR: Harvest House.

Ankerberg, J. and J. Weldon. 1999. *The Encyclopedia of Cults and New Religions*. Eugene, OR: Harvest House.

'Anti-Polygamy Standard'. 1881. *Anti-Polygamy Standard* 1, no. 12 (March): 4–5.

Antón, C. B. 2020. 'Coercive Persuasion As a Specific Type of Violence in Criminal Law'. *International Journal of Coercion, Abuse, and Manipulation* 1, no. 1: 61–72.

Atkins, G. G. 1923. *Modern Religious Cults and Movements*. New York: Fleming H. Revell.

Bacheler, O. 1838. *Mormonism Exposed, Internally and Externally*. New York: Author.

Barker, E. 1984. *The Making of a Moonie: Choice or Brainwashing?* London: Blackwell.

Bauer, W. 1971. *Orthodoxy and Heresy in Earliest Christianity*, translated by Philadelphia Seminar on Christian Origins. Edited by R. A. Kraft and G. Krodel. Mifflintown, PA: Sigler Press.

Beisner, E. C. 1998. *'Jesus Only' Churches*. Zondervan Guide to Cults and Religious Movements. Grand Rapids, MI: Zondervan.

Berger, H., ed. 2005. *Witchcraft and Magic: Contemporary North America.* Philadelphia: University of Pennsylvania Press.

Berger, P. L. 1967. *The Sacred Canopy: Elements of a Sociological Theory of Religion.* New York: Doubleday Anchor.

Berger, P. L. and T. Luckmann. 1966. *The Social Construction of Reality: A Treatise on the Sociology of Knowledge.* Harmondsworth: Penguin Books.

Bjornstad, J. 1979. *Counterfeits at Your Door.* Ventura, CA: Regal Books.

Boa, K. D. and R. A Bowman, Jr. 2001. *Faith Has Its Reasons: An Integrative Approach to Defending Christianity.* Colorado Springs, CO: NavPress.

Borovoy, A. A. 1988. *When Freedoms Collide: The Case for Our Civil Liberties.* Toronto: Lester & Orpen Dennys.

Bossick, K. 1983. 'The Godmakers: Film Produced by ex-Mormons Draws Crowds and a Lot of Controversy'. *The Idaho Statesman* (Boise), 11 December; photocopy reproduced in *Saints Alive in Jesus Newsletter* (January/February 1984): 5–10.

Bowman, R. 1994. *Jehovah's Witnesses.* Zondervan Guide to Cults and Religious Movements. Grand Rapids, MI: Zondervan.

Boyer, P. 1992. *When Time Shall Be No More: Prophecy Belief in American Culture.* Cambridge, MA: Harvard University Press.

Braden, C. S. 1949. *These Also Believe: A Study of Modern American Cults and Minority Religious Movements.* New York: Macmillan.

Branch, C. 1994. 'Witchcraft/Wicca'. *Watchman Fellowship Profile*; www.watchman.org/profiles/pdf/wiccaprofile.pdf, accessed 5 December 2022.

Bromley, D. G. and J. T. Richardson, eds. 1983. *The Brainwashing/Deprogramming Controversy: Sociological, Psychological, Legal and Historical Perspectives.* Studies in Religion and Society, vol. 5. New York: Edwin Mellen Press.

Bromley, D. G. and A. D. Shupe, Jr. 1981. *Strange Gods: The Great American Cult Scare.* Boston, MA: Beacon Press.

Bromley, D. G. and A. D. Shupe, Jr. 1987. 'The Future of the Anticult Movement'. In *The Future of New Religious Movements*, ed. D. G. Bromley and P. E. Hammond, 221–334. Macon, GA: Mercer University Press.

Brown, R. L. and R. Brown. 1981–95. *They Lie in Wait to Deceive: A Study in Anti-Mormon Deception.* 4 vols. Edited by B. Ellsworth. Mesa, AZ: Brownsworth.

Cameron, A. 2003. 'How to Read Heresiology'. *Journal of Medieval and Early Modern Studies* 33, no. 3: 471 92.

'Characteristics of Mormon Polygamy, No. IV'. 1881. *Anti-Polygamy Standard* 1, no. 11 (February): 2.

Chiniquy, C. 1880. *The Priest, the Woman, and the Confessional*. 43rd ed. New York: Fleming H. Revell.

Chiniquy, C. 1886. *Fifty Years in the Church of Rome*. New York: Fleming H. Revell.

Combs, G. H. 1899. *Some Latter-Day Religions*. Chicago, IL: Fleming H. Revell.

Cowan, D. E. 1991. *A Nakid Entent unto God: A Source/Commentary on* The Cloud of Unknowing. Wakefield, NH: Longwood Academic.

Cowan, D. E. 1999. 'Bearing False Witness: Propaganda, Reality-Maintenance, and Christian Anticult Apologetics', unpublished doctoral thesis, University of Calgary, Canada.

Cowan, D. E. 2002. 'Exits and Migrations: Foregrounding the Christian Counter-Cult'. *Journal of Contemporary Religion* 17, no. 3: 339–54.

Cowan, D. E. 2003a. *Bearing False Witness? An Introduction to the Christian Countercult*. Westport, CT: Praeger.

Cowan, D. E. 2003b. *The Remnant Spirit: Conservative Reform in Mainline Protestantism*. Westport, CT: Praeger.

Cowan, D. E. 2005a. 'Constructing the New Religious Threat: Countercult and Anticult Movements'. In *New Religious Movements: A Documentary Reader*, ed. D. Daschke and W. M. Ashcraft, 317–30. New York: New York University Press.

Cowan, D. E. 2005b. *Cyberhenge: Modern Pagans on the Internet*. New York: Routledge.

Cowan, D. E. 2006. 'The Evangelical Christian Countercult Movement'. In *Introduction to New and Alternative Religions in America: Histories and Controversies*, ed. E. V. Gallagher and W. M. Ashcroft, 143–64. Westport, CT: Greenwood Press.

Cowan, D. E. 2010. *Sacred Space: The Quest for Transcendence in Science Fiction Film and Television*. Waco, TX: Baylor University Press.

Cowan, D. E. 2016. 'The Christian Countercult Movement'. In *The Oxford Handbook of New Religious Movements*, ed. J. R. Lewis and I. B. Tøllefsen, 143–51. New York: Oxford University Press.

Cowan, D. E. 2018. *America's Dark Theologian: The Religious Imagination of Stephen King*. New York: New York University Press.

Cowan, D. E. 2020. 'Reading Religion in the Dead of Night'. In *Scared Sacred: Idolatry, Religion and Worship in the Horror Film*, ed. R. Booth, V. Griffiths, and E. Thompson, 7–15. Belfast: House of Leaves.

Cowan, D. E. 2022. *The Forbidden Body: Sex, Horror, and the Religious Imagination*. New York: New York University Press.

Cowan, D. E. Forthcoming. 'The Dangerous Cult Exercise: Popular Culture and the Ongoing Construction of the New Religious Threat'. In *'Cult'*

Rhetoric in the 21ˢᵗ Century: Deconstructing the Study of New Religious Movements, ed. E. Graham-Hyde and A. Thomas. London: Bloomsbury Academic.

Cowan, D. E. and D. G. Bromley. 2015. *Cults and New Religions: A Brief History*. Oxford: Wiley Blackwell.

Cross, F. L. and E. A. Livingstone, eds. 1983. *The Oxford Dictionary of the Christian Church*. Rev. ed. Oxford: Oxford University Press.

Cumbey, C. 1983. *Hidden Dangers of the Rainbow: The New Age Movement and Our Coming Age of Barbarism*. Rev. ed. Lafayette, LA: Huntingdon House.

Cyre, S. 1995. 'Truth Creates Boundaries'. *Theology Matters* 1, no. 2: 1–3.

Decker, J. E., prod. 1982. *The God Makers*. Written by J. E. Decker, D. Hunt and T. A. McMahon. Jeremiah Films.

DeMar, G. and P. Leithart. 1988. *The Reduction of Christianity: Dave Hunt's Theology of Cultural Surrender*. Atlanta, GA: American Vision.

DeStefano, A. 2018. *Inside the Atheist Mind: Unmasking the Religion of Those Who Say There Is No God*. Nashville, TN: Thomas Nelson.

Dhu, H. 1855. *Stanhope Burleigh: The Jesuits in Our Homes*. New York: Stringer & Townsend.

Di Marzio, R. 2020. '"People Trapped inside Shincheonji": Broadcasting the Darker Side of Deprogramming'. *Journal of CESNUR* 4, no. 3: 57–69.

'Doctrinal Statement on the Antichrist'. 2022. Wisconsin Evangelical Lutheran Synod; https://wels.net/about-wels/what-we-believe/doctrinal-statements/antichrist, accessed 11 December 2022.

Eco, U. 1980. *The Name of the Rose*. Translated by W. Weaver. New York: Alfred A. Knopf.

Edge, C. E. 2016. 'Why I Had to Escape a Fundamentalist Cult'. *ICSA Today* 7, no. 2; www.icsahome.com/articles/why-i-had-to-escape-a-fundamentalist-cult-doc, accessed 5 November 2022.

Enroth, R. 1977. *The Lure of the Cults*. Chappaqua, NY: Christian Herald Books.

Evangelical Ministries to Non-Christian Religions. 2022. 'Basic Beliefs'. *Evangelical Ministries to Non-Christian Religions*; https://emnr.org/about/the-lausanne-covenant, accessed 2 October 2022.

Eyerman, R. and A. Jamison. 1991. *Social Movements: A Cognitive Approach*. University Park: University of Pennsylvania Press.

Fautré, W. 2020a. *Coercive Change of Religion in South Korea: A Report on Kidnapping, Confinement and Forced De-conversion in South Korea*. Brussels: Human Rights without Frontiers.

Fautré, W. 2020b. 'Coercive Change of Religion in South Korea: The Case of Shincheonji Church'. *The Journal of CESNUR* 4, no. 3: 35–56.

Feil, E. 1992. 'From the Classical *Religio* to the Modern *Religion*: Elements of a Transformation between 1550 and 1650'. In *Religion in History: The Word, the Idea, the Reality*, ed. M. Depland and G. Vallée, 31–44. Waterloo, Canada: Wilfrid Laurier University Press.

Fluhman, J. S. 2012. *'A Peculiar People': Anti-Mormonism and the Making of Religion in Nineteenth-Century America*. Chapel Hill, NC: University of North Carolina Press.

Foster, J. M. 1894. *Christ the King*. Boston, MA: James H. Earle.

Foster, J. M. (1917) 1996. 'Rome, the Antagonist of the Nation'. In *The Fundamentals: A Testimony to the Truth*, vol. 3, ed. R. A. Torrey, A. C. Dixon et al., 301–14. Grand Rapids, MI: Baker Books.

Freed, J. 1980. *Moonwebs: Journey into the Mind of a Cult*. Toronto: Dorset.

Fresenborg, B. 1904. *'Thirty Years in Hell', or 'From Darkness to Light'*. St. Louis, MO: North-American Book House.

Froiseth, J. A., ed. 1887. *The Women of Mormonism: or The Story of Polygamy As Told by the Victims Themselves*. Detroit, MI: C. G. G. Paine.

Gardner, G. B. 1954. *Witchcraft Today*. London: Rider & Company.

Geisler, N. L. and R. Rhodes. 1997. *When Cultists Ask: A Popular Handbook on Cultic Misrepresentations*. Grand Rapids, MI: Baker Books.

George, L. 1995. *Crimes of Perception: An Encyclopedia of Heresies and Heretics*. New York: Paragon House.

Givens, T. L. 2013. *The Viper on the Hearth: Mormons, Myths, and the Construction of Heresy*. Rev. ed. New York: Oxford University Press.

Goldberg, L., ed. n.d. *Cult Recovery: A Clinician's Guide to Working with Former Members and Families*. Bonita Springs, FL: International Cultic Studies Association.

Gomes, A. 1998a. *Truth and Error: Comparative Charts of Cults and Christianity*. Zondervan Guide to Cults and Religious Movements. Grand Rapids, MI: Zondervan.

Gomes, A. 1998b. *Unitarian Universalism*. Zondervan Guide to Cults and Religious Movements. Grand Rapids, MI: Zondervan.

Green, J. 2011. 'Michele Bachmann's Church Says the Pope Is the Antichrist'. *The Atlantic* (13 July); www.theatlantic.com/politics/archive/2011/07/michele-bachmanns-church-says-the-pope-is-the-antichrist/241909, accessed December 13, 2022.

Griffin, S. M. 2004. *Anti-Catholicism and Nineteenth-Century Fiction*. Cambridge: Cambridge University Press.

Groothuis, D. 1986. *Unmasking the New Age*. Downers Grove, IL: InterVarsity Press.

Groothuis, D. (1988) 2015. *Confronting the New Age: How to Resist a Growing Religious Movement*. Reprint. Eugene, OR: Wipf & Stock.

Groothuis, D. 1990. *Revealing the New Age Jesus: Challenges to Orthodox Views of Christ*. Downers Grove, IL: InterVarsity Press.

Groothuis, R. 1996. *Are All Religions One?* Downers Grove, IL: InterVarsity Press.

Hadden, J. K. 1987. 'Toward Desacralizing Secularization Theory'. *Social Forces* 65, no. 3: 587–611.

Hahn, E. 2010. *How to Respond to Muslims*. 3rd ed. St. Louis, MO: Concordia Publishing House.

Hall, S. P. 2020. 'Being Mindful about Mindfulnesss: Exploring the Dark Side'. *International Journal of Coercion, Abuse, and Manipulation* 1, no. 1: 17–28.

Hanegraff, H. 2009. 'What Is a Religious Cult?' *Bible Answer Man* (radio); www.equip.org/perspectives/what-is-a-religious-cult, accessed 17 October 2022.

Hassan, S. 1990. *Combatting Cult Mind Control*. Rochester, VT: Park Street Press.

Hassan, S. 2000. *Releasing the Bonds: Empowering People to Think for Themselves*. Somerville, MA: Freedom of Mind Press.

Hawkins, C. 1998. *Goddess Worship, Witchcraft, and Neo-Paganism*. Zondervan Guide to Cults and Religious Movements. Grand Rapids, MI: Zondervan.

Hexham, I. and K. Poewe. 1997. *New Religions As Global Culture: Making the Human Sacred*: Boulder, CO: Westview Press.

Holley, T. and A. Kole. 1996. *Astrology and Psychic Phenomena*. Zondervan Guide to Cults and Religious Movements. Grand Rapids, MI: Zondervan.

'Housekeeper's Corner' 1881. *Anti-Polygamy Standard* 1, no. 11 (February): 2.

Howard, J., T. Fink., and N. Unseth 1990. *Confronting the Cultist in the New Age*. Old Tappan, NJ: Power Books.

Howe, E. D. 1834. *Mormonism Unvailed*. Plainsville, OH: Eber D. Howe.

Hunt, D. 1980. *The Cult Explosion*. Eugene, OR: Harvest House.

Hunt, D. 1983. *Peace, Prosperity, and the Coming Holocaust: The New Age Movement in Prophecy*. Eugene, OR: Harvest House.

Hunt, D. 1990. *Global Peace and the Rise of Antichrist*. Eugene, OR: Harvest House.

Hunt, D. 1991. 'A Cult Is a Cult'. *The Berean Call* (June): 1–2.

Hunt, D. 1994a. 'More on Being a Berean'. *The Berean Call* (February): 1–3.

Hunt, D. 1994b. *A Woman Rides the Beast: The Catholic Church and the Last Days*. Eugene, OR: Harvest House.

Hunt, D. 1996. *In Defense of the Faith: Biblical Answers to Challenging Questions*. Eugene, OR: Harvest House.

Hunt, D. 1998a. *Occult Invasion: The Subtle Seduction of World and Church.* Eugene, OR: Harvest House.

Hunt, D. 1998b. 'Q&A'. *The Berean Call* (August): 4.

Hunt, D. 1999. 'Q&A'. *The Berean Call* (March): 4.

Hunt, D. and E. Decker. 1984. *The Godmakers.* Eugene, OR: Harvest House.

Hunt, D. and T. A. McMahon. 1985. *The Seduction of Christianity: Spiritual Discernment in the Last Days.* Eugene, OR: Harvest House.

Hunt, D. and T. A. McMahon. 1987. *Beyond Seduction: A Return to Biblical Christianity.* Eugene, OR: Harvest House.

Hutton, R. 2019. *The Triumph of the Moon: A History of Modern Pagan Witchcraft.* Rev. ed. Oxford: Oxford University Press.

Hyla [J. D. Chaplin]. 1853. *The Convent and the Manse.* Cleveland, OH: John P. Jewett.

International Cultic Studies Association. n.d. 'Groups'. *International Cultic Studies Association*; www.icsahome.com/groups, accessed 5 October 2022.

Introvigne, M. 1993. 'Strange Bedfellows or Future Enemies?' *Update & Dialog on New Religious Movements* 3: 13–22.

Introvigne, M. 1995. 'The Secular Anti-Cult and the Religious Counter-Cult Movement: Strange Bedfellows or Future Enemies?' In *New Religions and the New Europe*, ed. R. Towler, 32–54. Aarhus, Denmark: RENNER Studies on New Religions.

Introvigne, M. 2021. 'Killing the Competition: Opposition to Shincheonji before and after the Covid-19 Crisis'. *Nova Religio* 25, no 1: 14–39.

Introvigne, M. 2022a. 'Afro-Brazilian Religions Targeted by Counter-cult Violence in Brazil'. *Bitter Winter: A Magazine on Religious Liberty and Human Rights* (29 September); https://bitterwinter.org/afro-brazilian-reli gions-targeted-in-brazil, accessed 1 December 2022.

Introvigne, M. 2022b. *Brainwashing: Myth or Reality?* Cambridge Elements in New Religious Movements. Cambridge: Cambridge University Press.

Introvigne, M. 2022c. 'Religious Intolerance in Brazil: Will Lulu Protect the Minorities?' *Bitter Winter: A Magazine on Religious Liberty and Human Rights* (3 November); https://bitterwinter.org/religious-intolerance-in-brazil, accessed 1 December 2022.

Irvine, W. C. 1935. *Heresies Exposed: A Brief Critical Examination in the Light of Holy Scriptures of Some of the Prevailing Heresies and False Teachings of Today.* New York: Loiseaux Bros.

James, W. (1902) 1999. *The Varieties of Religious Experience.* Reprint. New York: Modern Library.

Jones, P. and C. Matthews, eds. 1990. *Voices from the Circle: The Heritage of Western Paganism.* Wellingborough, UK: Aquarian Press.

Lalich, J. and M. Tobias. 2006. *Take Back Your Life: Recovering from Cults and Abusive Relationships*. Richmond, CA: Bay Tree.

Lambert, M. 1998. *The Cathars*. Oxford: Blackwell.

Langone, M. D. 1995. 'Secular and Religious Critiques of Cults: Complementary Visions, Not Irresolvable Conflicts'. *Cultic Studies Journal* 12, no. 2: 166–86.

Langone, M. D. 2015a. 'Characteristics Associated with Cultic Groups – Revised'. *ICSA Today* 6, no. 3: 10.

Langone, M. D. 2015b. 'The Definitional Ambiguity of Cult and ICSA's Mission'. *ICSA Today* 6, no. 3: 6–7.

Langone, M. D., ed. 1993. *Recovery from Cults: Help for Victims of Psychological and Spiritual Abuse*. New York: W. W. Norton.

Larson, B. 1969. *Hippies, Hindus, and Rock and Roll*. McCook, NE: Author.

Larson, B. 1989. *Larson's New Book of Cults*. Wheaton, IL: Tyndale House.

Larson, B. 1999. *Larson's Book of Spiritual Warfare*. Nashville, TN: Thomas Nelson.

Larson, B. 2011. *Demon-Proofing Prayers: Bob Larson's Guide to Winning Spiritual Warfare*. Shippensburg, PA: Destiny Image.

Larson, B. 2016. *Dealing with Demons: An Introductory Guide to Exorcism and Discerning Evil Spirits*. Shippensburg, PA: Destiny Image.

Larson, B. and L. Larson. 2017. *Set Your Family Free: Breaking Demonic Assignments against Your Household*. Shippensburg, PA: Destiny Image.

Lea, H. C. 1906. *A History of the Inquisition of the Middle Ages*. 3 vols. New York: Macmillan.

Leakhead. 2020. Review of *The God Makers*. Internet Movie Database (16 August); www.imdb.com/title/tt1791631, accessed 10 September 2022.

Lee, R. and E. Hindson. 1993. *Angels of Deceit: The Masterminds behind Religious Deception*. Eugene, OR: Harvest House.

Lewis, G. R. 1966. *Confronting the Cults*. Phillipsburg, NJ: Presbyterian and Reformed.

Livesey, R. 1838. *An Exposure of Mormonism, Being a Statement of Facts relating to the Self-Styled 'Latter-day Saints', and the Origins of the Book of Mormon*. Preston, UK: J. Livesey.

Lockwood, R. P., ed. 2000. *Anti-Catholicism in American Culture*. Huntingdon, IN: Our Sunday Visitor.

Lucas, P. C. and T. Robbins, ed. 2004. *New Religious Movements in the Twenty-First Century: Legal, Political, and Social Challenges in Global Perspective*. New York: Routledge.

Lüdemann, G. and M. Janssen. 1997. *Suppressed Prayers: Gnostic Spirituality in Early Christianity*, trans. J. Bowden. Harrisburg, PA: Trinity House.

Lutzer, E. W. and J. F. DeVries. 1989. *Satan's 'Evangelistic' Strategy for This New Age*. Grand Rapids, MI: Chosen Books.

Mannheim, K. 1952. 'The Problem of a Sociology of Knowledge'. In *Essays on the Sociology of Knowledge*, by K. Mannheim, ed. P. Kekcskemeti, 134–90. London: Routledge & Kegan Paul.

Marrs. T. 1990. *Texe Marrs Book of New Age Cults and Religions*. Austin, TX: Living Truth.

Marsden, G. M. (1980) 2022. *Fundamentalism and American Culture: The Shaping to Twentieth-Century Evangelicalism, 1870–1925*. 3rd ed. New York: Oxford University Press.

Martin, P. R. 1993. *Cult-Proofing Your Kids*. Grand Rapids, MI: Zondervan.

Martin, W. R., Jr. 1955. *The Rise of the Cults: An Introductory Guide to the Non-Christian Cults*. Grand Rapids, MI: Zondervan.

Martin, W. R., Jr. 1965. *The Kingdom of the Cults: An Analysis of the Major Cult Systems in the Present Christian Era*. London: Marshall, Morgan & Scott. (Revised: Minneapolis, MN: Bethany House, 1977, 1985, 1997).

Martin, W. R., Jr. 1976. *Mormonism*. Minneapolis, MN: Bethany House.

Martin, W. R., Jr. 1980. *Rise of the Cults: A Quick Guide to the Cults*. 3rd ed. Santa Ana, CA: Vision House.

Martin, W. R., Jr. 2019. *The Kingdom of the Cults: The Definitive Work on the Subject*. 6th ed. K. Rische and J. M. Rische. Minneapolis, MN: Bethany House.

Martin, W. R. Jr., J. M. Rische, and K. van Gorden. 2008. *The Kingdom of the Occult*. Nashville, TN: Thomas Nelson.

Mather, G. and L. A. Nichols. 1995. *Masonic Lodge*. Zondervan Guide to Cults and Religious Movements. Grand Rapids, MI: Zondervan.

Matrisciana, C. 1985. *Gods of the New Age*. Eugene, OR: Harvest House.

Mattison, H. 1846. *Scriptural Defence of the Doctrine of the Trinity, or a Check to Modern Arianism, As Taught By Campbellites, Hicksites, New Lights, Universalists and Mormons; and especially by a Sect calling themselves 'Christians'*. New York: Lewis Colby and Company.

M'Chesney, J. 1838. *An Antidote to Mormonism; A Warning Voice to the Church and Nation; The Purity of Christian Principles Defended; And Truth Disentangled from Error*. New York: Author.

McDowell, J. and D. Stewart. 1983. *Handbook of Today's Religions*. San Bernardino, CA: Here's Life.

McFarland, A. 2012. *10 Answers for Atheists: How to Have an Intelligent Conversation about the Existence of God*. Ada, MI: Bethany House.

McMahon, T. A. 2000. 'Mary Who?' *The Berean Call* (September): 5–6.

McMahon, T. A. 2018. 'Biblically Thinking about Catholicism: Tradition vs. Scripture'. Bend, OR: The Berean Call.

McNiece, R. G. (1917) 1996. 'Mormonism: Its Origin, Characteristics and Doctrines'. In *The Fundamentals: A Testimony to the Truth*, vol. 4, ed. R. A. Torrey, A. C. Dixon et al., 131–48. Grand Rapids, MI: Baker Books.

Medhurst, T. W. (1917) 1996. 'Is Romanism Christianity?' In *The Fundamentals: A Testimony to the Truth*, vol. 3, ed. R. A. Torrey, A. C. Dixon et al., 288–300. Grand Rapids, MI: Baker Books.

Melton, J. G. 2006. 'Critiquing Cults: An Historical Perspective'. In *Introduction to New and Alternative Religions in America: Histories and Controversies*, ed. E. V. Gallagher and W. M. Ashcraft, 126–42. Westport, CT: Greenwood Press.

Miller, D. 2012. *Emancipating the World: A Christian Response to Radical Islam and Fundamentalist Atheism*. Seattle, WA: Youth With a Mission.

Miller, T., ed. 1995. *America's Alternative Religions*. Albany: State University of New York Press.

'Mission Statement'. n.d. *Watchman Fellowship*; www.watchman.org/about-us/mission-statement, accessed 3 December 2022.

Monk, M. (1836) 1876. *Awful Disclosures of Maria Monk, As Exhibited in a Narrative of Her Sufferings during Her Residence of Five Years As a Novice and Two Years As a Black Nun in the Hotel Dieu Nunnery, at Montréal, Ont.* Rev. ed. New York: Truth Seeker Company.

Monk, M. 1837. *Further Disclosures of Maria Monk, Concerning the Hotel Dieu Nunnery of Montréal; also, Her Visit to Nun's Island and Disclosures Concerning That Secret Retreat*. Boston, MA: Leavitt, Lord.

Moorehead, W. G. (1917) 1996. 'Millennial Dawn: A Counterfeit of Christianity'. In *The Fundamentals: A Testimony to the Truth*, vol. 4, ed. R. A. Torrey, A. C. Dixon et al., 109–30. Grand Rapids, MI: Baker Books.

Morey, R. A. 1980. *How to Answer a Jehovah's Witness*. Minneapolis, MN: Bethany Fellowship.

Morey, R. A. 2015. *Is Eastern Orthodoxy Christian?* Maitland, FL: Xulon Press.

Muck, T. 1990. *Alien Gods on American Turf: How World Religions Are Evangelizing Your Neighborhood*. Wheaton, IL: Victor Books.

National Conference of Christians and Jews. 1984. *Programs in Pluralism* (March/April): n.p.

Nietzsche, F. (1895) 1990. *The Twilight of the Idols/The Anti-Christ*. Reprint. Translated by R. J. Hollingdale. London: Penguin Classics.

Novak, G. n.d. 'Worst of the Anti-Mormon Web Special Edition: Does James White Have a Genuine Doctorate?' *Scholarly & Historical Information*

Exchange for Latter-day Saints; www.shields-research.org/Novak/james.htm, accessed 4 December 2022.

Numbers, R. L. 1992. *The Creationists: The Evolution of Scientific Creationism*. Berkeley: University of California Press.

O'Gorman, E. 1871. *Convent Life Unveiled: Trials and Persecutions of Edith O'Gorman, Otherwise Sister Teresa de Chantal, of St. Joseph's Convent, Hudson, N.J.* Hartford, CT: Connecticut Publishing.

'Our History'. 2022. *Christian Research Institute*; www.equip.org/about/our-history, accessed 20 November 2022.

Pagels, E. 1989. *The Gnostic Gospels*. New York: Vintage Books.

Parsons, T. 1841. *Mormon Fanaticism Exposed. A Compendium of the Book of Mormon, or Joseph Smith's Golden Bible. Also, the Examination of Its Internal and External Evidences, with the Arguments to Refute Its Pretences to a Revelation from God: Argued before the Free Discussion Society in the City of Boston, July, 1841, between Elder Freeman Nickerson, a Mormon, and the Author, Tyler Parsons*. Boston, MA: Author.

Passantino, B. and G. Passantino. 1990a. 'What Is a Cult?'; www.answers.org/cultsandreligions/what_is_a_cult, accessed 12 September 2022.

Passantino, B. and G. Passantino. 1990b. *Witch Hunt*. Nashville, TN: Thomas Nelson.

Passantino, B. and G. Passantino. 1991. *When the Devil Dares Your Kids: Protecting Your Children from Satanism, Witchcraft, and the Occult*. Ann Arbor, MI: Servant Books.

Passantino, B. and G. Passantino. 1995. *Satanism*. Zondervan Guide to Cults and Religious Movements. Grand Rapids, MI: Zondervan.

Passantino, G. 1997. 'Critiquing Cult Mind-Control Model'. In *Kingdom of the Cults*, ed. H. Hanegraaf, 49–78. Minneapolis, MN: Bethany House.

Paulk, E. 1987. *That the World May Know*. N.p.: K-Dimension.

Peretti, F. 1986. *This Present Darkness*. Wheaton, IL: Crossway Books.

Peretti, F. 1989. *Piercing the Darkness*. Wheaton, IL: Crossway Books.

Pollock, A. J. (1917) 1996. 'Modern Spiritualism Briefly Tested by Scripture'. In *The Fundamentals: A Testimony to the Truth*, vol. 4, ed. R. A. Torrey, A. C. Dixon et al., 166–82. Grand Rapids, MI: Baker Books.

Reed. R. T. 1835. *Six Months in a Convent, or, The Narrative of Rebecca Theresa Reed, Who Was under the Influence of the Roman Catholics about Two Years, and an Inmate of the Ursuline Convent on Mount Benedict, Charlestown, Mass., Nearly Six Months, in the Years 1831–2*. Boston, MA: Russell, Odiorne & Metcalf.

Reid, T. F., and M. Virkler. 1986. *Seduction? A Biblical Response*. Wilmington, PA: Son-rise.

Religious Analysis Service. n.d. 'Religious Analysis Service Articles of Incorporation and Bylaws (1946)'; www.ras.org/about-us, accessed 2 October 2022.

Rhodes, R. 1993. *Reasoning from the Scriptures with the Jehovah's Witnesses*. Eugene, OR: Harvest House.

Rhodes, R. 1994. *The Culting of America*. Eugene, OR: Harvest House.

Rhodes, R. 1995. *Reasoning from the Scriptures with Mormons*. Eugene, OR: Harvest House.

Rhodes, R. 1997. *The Complete Book of Bible Answers*. Eugene, OR: Harvest House.

Rhodes, R. 2000. *Reasoning from the Scriptures with Catholics*. Eugene, OR: Harvest House.

Rhodes, R. 2001. *Reasoning from the Scriptures with the Jehovah's Witnesses*. 2nd ed. Eugene, OR: Harvest House.

Rhodes, R. 2002. *Reasoning from the Scriptures with Muslims*. Eugene, OR: Harvest House.

Richardson, J. T. 2011. 'Deprogramming: From Private Self-Help to Governmental Organized Repression'. *Crime, Law and Social Change* 55, no. 4: 321–36.

Roberts, R. P. 2000. 'Are Evangelism, Mission, and Apologetics a Hate Crime?' *Watchman Fellowship*; www.watchman.org/articles/other-religious-topics/are-evangelism-missions-and-apologetics-a-hate-crime, accessed 13 December 2022.

Scharffs, G. W. 1989. *The Truth about 'The Godmakers'*. 2nd ed. Salt Lake City, UT: Publishers Press.

Schultz, N. L. 2000. *Fire and Roses: The Burning of the Charlestown Convent, 1834*. New York: Free Press.

Scott, L. C. 1993. *Why We Left a Cult: Six People Tell Their Stories*. Grand Rapids, MI: Baker Books.

Shlemon, A. 2019. 'Arguments Don't Have to Be Argumentative'. YouTube video, 0.59, posted by Stand to Reason, 14 January; www.youtube.com/watch?v=ncCtfgdxnmQ, accessed 6 November 2022.

Shlemon, A. 2020. 'Apologetics Isn't Argumentative'. *Stand to Reason* (7 April); www.str.org/w/apologetics-isn-t-argumentative, accessed 3 November 2022.

Shlemon, A. 2022. 'Evangelism Isn't Disrespectful'. *Stand to Reason* (15 November); www.str.org/w/evangelism-isn-t-disrespectful, accessed 16 November 2022.

Shupe, A. D., Jr. and D. G. Bromley. 1980. *The New Vigilantes: Deprogrammers, Anti-Cultists, and the New Religions*. Sage Library of Social Research, vol. 113. Beverly Hills, CA: Sage.

Shupe, A. D., Jr. and D. G. Bromley. 1995. 'The Evolution of Modern American Anticult Ideology: A Case Study in Frame Extension'. In *America's Alternative Religions*, ed. T. Miller, 411–16. Albany: State University of New York Press.

Shupe, A. D., D. G. Bromley, and D. L. Oliver. 1984. *The Anti-Cult Movement in America: A Bibliography and Historical Survey*. New York: Garland.

Shupe, A. D., R. Spielmann, and S. Stigall. 1977. 'Deprogramming: The New Exorcism'. In *Conversion Careers: In and Out of the New Religions*, ed. J. T. Richardson, 145–60. Sage Contemporary Social Science Issues, vol. 47. Beverly Hills, CA: Sage.

Singer, M. T. and Lalich, J. 1995. *Cults in Our Midst: The Hidden Menace in Our Everyday Lives*. San Francisco, CA: Jossey-Bass.

Slick, M. 2002. *Right Answers for Wrong Beliefs*. Tonbridge, UK: Sovereign World.

Smith, K. A. 2021. 'The Sin of Heresy: Opposition to Heresy in Augustine's *Confessions*'. *Heythrop Journal*; https://doi-org.proxy.lib.uwaterloo.ca/10.1111/heyj.13980, accessed 10 September 2022.

Spencer, J. R. 1986. *Have You Witnessed to a Mormon Lately?* Grand Rapids, MI: Chosen Books.

Spencer, J. R. 1993. *Heresy Hunters: Character Assassination in the Church*. Lafayette, LA: Huntingdon House.

Stand to Reason. 2022. 'Mission, Vision, and Values'. *Stand to Reason*; www.str.org/mission-and-values, accessed 15 November 2022.

Stark, R. and W. S. Bainbridge. 1985. *The Future of Religion: Secularization, Revival, and Cult Formation*. Berkeley: University of California Press.

Stark, R. and W. S. Bainbridge. 1997. *Religion, Deviance, and Social Control*. New York: Routledge.

'Statement of Faith'. 2022. *Stand to Reason*; www.str.org/statement-of-faith, accessed 7 December 2022.

Sunderland, L. 1838. *Mormonism Exposed and Refuted*. New York: Piercy & Reed, Printers.

Tobias, M. and J. Lalich. 1994. *Captive Hearts, Captive Minds: Freedom from Cults and Abusive Relationships*. Alameda, CA: Hunter House.

Torrey, R. A. (1917) 1996. 'Preface'. In *The Fundamentals: A Testimony to the Truth*, ed. R. A. Torrey, A. C. Dixon et al. 4 vols. Grand Rapids, MI: Baker Books.

Trollope, F. M. 1847. *Father Eustace: A Tale of the Jesuits*. 3 vols. London: Henry Colburn.

'Updates'. 2022. *Centers for Apologetics Research*; https://thecenters.org/updates.aspx, accessed 3 December 2022.

Valiente, D. 1973. *An ABC of Witchcraft: Past and Present.* New York: St. Martin's Press.

Van Baalen, J. K. 1960. *The Chaos of Cults: A Study in Present-day Isms.* 3rd rev. ed. Grand Rapids, MI: Eerdmans.

Wakefield, W. L. and A. P. Evans. 1991. *Heresies of the Middle Ages: Selected Sources Translated and Annotated.* New York: Columbia University Press.

Watters, R. 1987. *Refuting Jehovah's Witnesses.* Manhattan Beach, CA: Bethel Ministries.

Welter, B. 1987. 'From Maria Monk to Paul Blanschard: A Century of Protestant Anti-Catholicism'. In *Uncivil Religion: Interreligious Hostility in America*, ed. R. Bellah and F. Greenspan, 43–72. New York: Crossroad.

'What We Do'. n.d. *Mormonism Research Ministry*; www.mrm.org/about, accessed 6 December 2022.

White, James R. 1990. *The Fatal Flaw: Do the Teachings of Roman Catholicism Deny the Gospel.* Southbridge, MA: Crowne.

White, James R. 1998. *Mary: Another Redeemer?* Minneapolis, MN: Bethany House.

Wilber, K. 1993. *The Spectrum of Consciousness.* 2nd ed. Wheaton, IL: Quest Books.

Williams, B. 1997. *The ABC of Cults.* Ross-shire, UK: Christian Focus.

Williams, R. 2001. *Arius: Heresy and Tradition.* Rev. ed. Grand Rapids, MI: Eerdmans.

Wilson, M. E. (1917) 1996. 'Eddyism, Commonly Called "Christian Science"'. In *The Fundamentals: A Testimony to the Truth*, vol. 4, R. A. Torrey, A. C. Dixon et al., 149–65. Grand Rapids, MI: Baker Books.

Winchester, B. 1841. *Plain Facts, Shewing the Origin of the Spaulding Story, concerning the Manuscript Found, and Its Being Transformed into the Book of Mormon; with a Short Biography of Dr. P. Hulbert, the Author of Said Story; Thereby Proving to Every Lover of Truth, beyond the Possibility of Successful Contradiction, That the Said Story was a Base Fabrication, without Even a Shadow of Truth.* Bedford, MA: C. B. Merry.

Wise, R. 1986. *The Church Divided: The Holy Spirit and a Spirit of Seduction.* South Plainfield, NJ: Bridge.

Yamamoto, J. I. 1998. *Buddhism, Taoism, and Other Far Eastern Religions.* Zondervan Guide to Cults and Religious Movements. Grand Rapids, MI: Zondervan.

Acknowledgements

Although I have gone on in my own career to consider very different approaches to the enduring problem of the religious imagination (e.g., Cowan 2010, 2018, 2022), I am grateful that producing this volume has given me the opportunity to look back on an earlier part of that journey. And, in light of this, it seems only appropriate to dedicate these efforts to two of those who walked it with me, my mentors, Jeffrey K. Hadden and Irving R. Hexham.

Cambridge Elements ⁼

New Religious Movements

Founding Editor
†James R. Lewis

Wuhan University

The late James R. Lewis was Professor of Philosophy at Wuhan University, China. He served as the editor or co-editor for four book series, was the general editor for the *Alternative Spirituality and Religion Review*, and the associate editor for the *Journal of Religion and Violence*. His publications include *The Cambridge Companion to Religion and Terrorism* (Cambridge University Press 2017) and *Falun Gong: Spiritual Warfare and Martyrdom* (Cambridge University Press 2018).

Series Editor
Rebecca Moore

San Diego State University

Rebecca Moore is Emerita Professor of Religious Studies at San Diego State University. She has written and edited numerous books and articles on Peoples Temple and the Jonestown tragedy. Publications include *Beyond Brainwashing: Perspectives on Cultic Violence* (Cambridge University Press 2018) and *Peoples Temple and Jonestown in the Twenty-First Century* (Cambridge University Press 2022).

About the Series
Elements in New Religious Movements go beyond cult stereotypes and popular prejudices to present new religions and their adherents in a scholarly and engaging manner. Case studies of individual groups, such as Transcendental Meditation and Scientology, provide in-depth consideration of some of the most well-known, and controversial, groups. Thematic examinations of women, children, science, technology, and other topics focus on specific issues unique to these groups. Historical analyses locate new religions in specific religious, social, political, and cultural contexts. These examinations demonstrate why some groups exist in tension with the wider society and why others live peaceably in the mainstream. The series highlights the differences, as well as the similarities, within this great variety of religious expressions. To discuss contributing to this series please contact Professor Moore, remoore@sdsu.edu.

Cambridge Elements $\equiv$

New Religious Movements

Elements in the Series

A full series listing is available at: www.cambridge.org/ENRM

Printed in the United States
by Baker & Taylor Publisher Services